Y

as you feel

Dumb &

not anymore

Depressed

only if you let it.

PIXII WILLIAMS

LET THE F*CK GO

Cover design by Anze Ban V
Edited by KAA, Adam Strange
Headshots by Lydia Victoria
Published by Pixii Williams
Images By Canva Magic Studio

Disclaimer:
This book is designed to provide informational and educational content. It is not intended to replace professional advice, including but not limited to medical, psychological, legal, or financial guidance. Pixii Williams, the author of this book, holds a Level 2 qualification in mental health and is a certified life coach. However, she is not a licensed therapist and does not offer therapy services.
The author and publisher cannot be held responsible for any actions, decisions, or consequences taken by readers based on the material within this book. Readers are encouraged to seek professional advice when appropriate.

This book is meant to inspire, guide, and support readers on their journey toward personal growth, but it is not a guarantee of specific results. Each individual's path and experience will differ.

Acknowledgements:
I would like to thank Christopher Snell, Jackie Clark, Ken Williams, Adam Williams, Jane Goodman, Ellen Bentley, Samantha Bishop and Betty Clark for their unwavering support and inspiration throughout this journey. Your guidance and belief in this project have been invaluable.

For more information, visit my social media platforms for coaching, community, and the latest updates.

@pixiiwilliams

Acknowledgements

To my Auntie Netty and my little kitten, Peaches. Losing you both was a tough reminder of just how short life really is. You've taught me to stop holding back and start living fully. Your love, lessons, and memories stay with me every day, reminding me to make the most of every moment and live life on my own terms. Thank you for everything, and you'll always be a part of my journey.

To my mum, who never gave up no matter what life threw at her, the struggles you've faced and how you've handled them have taught me the incredible power of the mind and resilience. You believed in me when I lost the ability to believe in myself. You encouraged me even when you felt I wasn't on the path that aligned with me. You've always made me feel like the strong, powerful woman I am. Even though our past has been filled with hardship, trauma, and pain, you managed to hold it all together for me. You are the strongest, most incredible woman I know, and I'm so grateful for everything you've done for me. I wouldn't be the woman I am today without your unconditional love.

To my dad, thank you for supporting every business idea and endeavour I've had and for believing in me even when I struggled to believe in myself. Your past has taught me more than you'll ever know, giving me a deeper understanding of how our backgrounds condition us. Life hasn't been easy for you, yet you've still managed to give me and my brother, Adam Williams, so much love and support. Though we're so similar yet worlds apart, I know you're proud of me, and I want you to know I'm so proud of you, too. Thank you for your financial support and your unwavering love.

And finally, to my ride-or-die, my best friend and soulmate, Christopher Snell, what you've done for me will never be forgotten. If it weren't for you, achieving my goals and aspirations would've been impossible. You believed in me, cheered me on, and supported me emotionally and financially. I never thought I'd meet someone who understands me as much as you do. Thank you for picking me up when I fell, for loving me unconditionally, and for being my biggest supporter. You're the biggest reason I was able to overcome the lifelong depression that was consuming me, and for that, I love you so much. Thank you.

And last of all, I want to thank myself for never giving up, even when I wanted to, for continuing to push forward when the world felt like it was too much.

To all my supporters on social media: In 2024, I started a TikTok page to help, guide, and inspire people. Three months later, not only did I build a following of over 10k people and create a beautiful community, but I also launched my online coaching platform, *Thrive Beyond Limits*. To all the Thrivers: You keep me accountable and feed my soul every day. Helping, guiding, motivating, and supporting you through my coaching is one of the greatest honours of my life.

CONTENTS

INTRODUCTION

Welcome, my beautiful humans! This book is here to guide you through life. It's perfect for anyone just beginning their self-development journey or wanting to see life from a fresh perspective. Inside, you'll find the knowledge and tools to help you live a happier, more stress-free life. I've spent the last ten years on my own journey, diving into powerful, inspirational books, some over 100 years old. Now, don't get me wrong, these books hold priceless wisdom, but they can be tricky to understand, especially if you're a neurodivergent human like me. I've created this book to be accessible to everyone, breaking down the oldest self-help methods into simple, practical steps you can actually use.

Since I was a child, I've dealt with depression, anxiety, overthinking, constant worrying, you name it, all the habits and traits that keep us stuck. But with the help of books, coaches, mentors and the life lessons we all get thrown at us, I managed to pull myself out of those low-vibrational energies and all the self-destructive talk. Now, I live a life of fulfilment, growth and true understanding of who I am and what I genuinely want from my life. I'm confident in sharing how I broke free from those patterns and thought spirals, and I'm here to show you how you can, too.

I hope you understand you are not alone, weird, different, or helpless. The struggles we face in our lives make us stronger and shape us into the beautiful individuals we are.

It's not wrong to want a little help along the way. During our time together in this book, if you come across something that triggers you, please pay attention to why it's triggering you. I'm not here to put you down or criticise you in any way; my purpose is to assist you in achieving a better life and developing a mindset that will help you find happiness, alignment, individuality, and success. I want you to know that I'm not perfect. I still have my moments when I sometimes think the worst of situations. The one thing that allows me to be grateful and grounded, what keeps me happy, free and calm, is the pure and undeniable fact that tomorrow is not promised.

I understand we're all different humans, going through different experiences. I cannot tell you exactly what to do in your life, but I can guide you. I haven't walked in your shoes nor you in mine, but I know I was hitting rock bottom every day for years and with the right tools and knowledge, I got myself out of that.

I know you can do the same.

I know what it feels like to lose hope, to feel like there's no point that no one truly gets you. But here's the truth: no one needs to understand you except you. Like so many, I had to unlearn, recondition and teach myself to become a genuinely happier and more grateful person. Growing up, I faced my share of trauma, anger, and all the negative conditioning that comes with it. Generations of ancestral pain, years of silenced voices, suppressed emotions, and inherited struggles get woven into our DNA. But we don't have to stay bound by it.

But what if I told you I could make your life easier? What if I said I could change how you see the whole world in this book? What if waking up every day wasn't a chore; it was a blessing?
Because the simple fact is, if we do not understand how the mind works, why we have certain thoughts and why we think or act in ways that do not serve us, long-lasting change will not occur.

Trust me, I can help you.

Through our journey together, I will show you that not everyone is conditioned to be 'happy. ' This lack of conditioning leads to lifelong suffering... if you allow it to. We will all have hardships during our life, but stressing or worrying about it will not change the fact that life throws some pretty sh*t stuff at us sometimes. But embracing everything and allowing hardship to shape us and teach us what we cannot learn in books removes the victim and blame factor.

I understand you; I get it.
You've got this!

'Thoughts are like seeds; they must be sown, fed and watered. In this book, we will plant some, and your job is to remember they are there, nurture them and watch them grow by regularly reminding yourself about the information in this book.'

HUNGRY FOR ANSWERS

'Books don't just tell stories; they teach us how to write our own.'

I want to start off by saying that I was right where you are now, hungry for answers and success but, more importantly, happiness. I didn't understand my mind until I started reading books; they truly changed my life.

My mum always encouraged me to read when I was younger. She'd say, "If I can't help you myself, I'll find other ways to help you." But being a grumpy, 'misunderstood' teenager (aren't they all), I would turn my nose up at the idea. The shortened version is that I'm dyslexic, and for my whole childhood, I was told, 'You CAN'T read properly' by adults like tutors, parents and specialists. The reason behind the capitals is that they are the only words the universe, god, mother nature and or our subconsciouses can hear.

The 'CAN'T.'

I believed I couldn't read, so whenever I tried, I would get extremely frustrated and even cry at times. What I now realise, without trying, is that the people around me planted this limiting statement in my head that I carried with me for years.

Who knew the power of word or thought could be so strong?

I am not saying that the adults in my life purposely played a part in my underachieving in school. My point is that the words we use when talking to ourselves and to others can warp our reality.

After leaving university, I was through with hitting rock bottom every week, so I finally took my mother's advice and started reading self-help and development books. Slowly, I started to realise that I could read and not half as bad as I thought. The more I read, the more powerful I felt; knowledge really is power.

'The most important moment is right this very second, something we will never get back.'

So, what I mean by this is that the most important moment we have is always right at this very second. Our most valuable asset is time. Time is something we will never get back; it comes and goes quicker than a blink of an eye.

Some of you might think, "I have a scattered brain", or "I can't stop overthinking". It's ok, I understand. I have been there, and sometimes, the overthinking will come back.

We're only human, right? We have up to 80,000 thoughts a day- crazy, isn't it? Most of these are on autopilot, like knowing how to drive, walk, or talk without thinking too hard. But here's the crazy thing: 80% of our thoughts are repetitive. That's because of our conditioning, which can either hype us up or totally bring us down.

Our thoughts are deeply tied to our emotions. When we're stressed, happy, or excited, our brain starts firing off thoughts to try and make sense of what we're feeling.

On top of that, our minds are constantly on the lookout for danger, a habit built into us from way back when we were part of the animal kingdom. It's just our brain's way of trying to keep us safe. Pretty cool, huh?
But it's also something we can learn to work with instead of against.

WE ARE HUMAN, and the most important thing is to go easy on yourself (whilst having some sort of structure and balance). Have fun, do what you enjoy, and do things simply because you love doing them.

When we live out of alignment with our true selves, life becomes a struggle, an effort and unenjoyable.

So the question is, how do we live in alignment?
By doing things you love to do, for example:

- feeling at peace
- being fulfilled
- having fun
- feeling empowered
- communicating with yourself
- moving your body

In this book, I will guide you through helpful tools that empower you to truly love and enjoy life while creating lasting, meaningful change.

The aim isn't to be 'perfect' all day, every day, or constantly positive. The aim is to acknowledge when you are being negative, moody, low, self-destructive or any of the other emotions we face as humans and then shift your focus.

Let me say that again.

'The aim is not to be perfect all day, every day. It's to acknowledge when you are being negative, moody or low and then shift your focus.'

Just remember: it's okay; everyone is different, and everyone has their own way of escaping from their mental funk. I can only help by guiding, asking questions, and explaining my own story. I haven't walked in your shoes nor you in mine, so what worked for me might not work for you.

I am here to open your mind, show you another perspective on life and help you trust your inner voice, as you are truly the only person who has the answers that you have been looking for.

For many years, I have been searching for answers from others, only to realise that the information and knowledge I was searching for were within me. We just have to unlock the answers in our minds, as no one else can tell you what answers we seek.

Have trust in yourself, I promise you've got this! This is what your intuition is for; some people call it our 'higher self', and in life, much of our conditioning from childhood has taught us not to follow or listen to our intuition. This creates mind overload when making 'logical decisions' instead of making the ones that truly feel 'right' for you personally.

Please feel free to do the exercises and answer the questions I give you as we go. It may feel weird, uncomfortable or out of place to do so, but as Einstein said:

'Insanity is doing the same thing over and over again and expecting different results.'

Einstein himself was also dyslexic; there is truly no limit but your mind.

Here are some great ways to start helping, healing, getting focused, aligned and building a relationship with yourself:

1.   Journaling

Journaling is a powerful practice that allows you to regularly express your thoughts, feelings and experiences, as well as reflect on past events. It's a simple but incredibly impactful tool for self-expression, self-awareness, and personal growth. People use journaling in many different ways, depending on their goals, but at its core, it helps with processing and organising thoughts, emotions, and ideas.

2. Visualisation

Visualisation is the practice of creating mental images or visual representations of goals, outcomes, or desired situations in your mind. It's a technique often used to enhance motivation, improve performance, and help achieve personal or professional goals. One way to visualise is by imagining yourself succeeding or experiencing positive outcomes. Visualisation can also help align your thoughts and behaviours with what you want to achieve.

3. Dancing, Moving and Music

Music and dance, or simply moving your body, play a crucial role in personal development for various reasons, as they influence both your physical and mental well-being. It allows you to connect with yourself on a deeper level, release emotions, and enhance creativity and self-expression.

4. Gratitude

Gratitude is the practice of acknowledging and valuing the positive aspects of life, whether they are significant or small. It involves deliberately concentrating on the things you are grateful for, which can vary from materialistic objects, health, family, or money flow. Through consistently practising gratitude, you change your perspective from focusing on what you don't have to appreciating what is already in your life.

Remember, we are all different; not every point will resonate with you, and that's okay. But one thing to embrace is gratitude because it truly is the key to happiness.

Why? Because when we begin to notice and become aware of the many things in our lives we're grateful for, we shift the script from wanting and needing more to genuinely appreciating what we already have. You cannot feel ungrateful and grateful at the same time, and that's why gratitude itself will always bring you happiness.

When we're stuck in a state of, *"I want more," "What I'm doing isn't good enough,"* or *"I must be better,"* we're operating from a mindset of lack, of *not enough and when* we're in that state of *not enough*, the universal law, often called the Law of Attraction, reflects it right back at us. This principle is simple: what you focus on expands. If you focus on what you lack, you'll attract more lack. When we shift into gratitude, celebrate our wins, acknowledge our progress, and truly embrace the good feelings when they come, we change the game.

Being thankful for the things and people we already have in our lives sends out a powerful message. And by that same law, we open ourselves up to receiving even more abundance.

When working on your personal development, it's important to understand who you are and how you truly feel. That is the first step!

Grab a pen and notebook, or simply reflect on these questions and explore what it feels like to live a life that truly aligns with who you are:

1. What does happiness look like to me?
Examples: spending time with my family, going out with friends, playing music, writing, making money, working and helping others.

2. What would I do if I could do anything with my life?
Examples: set up a charity, start a business, be a stay-at-home parent, work for a company or look after animals.

3. What does success mean to me?
Examples: working remotely, healing, travelling, owning a big business, owning a small business, being a millionaire, having enough to pay the bills, spending time with family or even living off-grid.

Please note that there are no wrong or right answers to these questions; every human is different, and that's the beauty of life. Wrong or right are just perspectives. Just like these questions, there is no good, bad, wrong, or right.

So, why is it so important to ask ourselves these questions? If we don't know how we want to spend our time here on earth, then how will we achieve happiness? How will we aim if there's nowhere to shoot?

'Many people think the answer is to think, but the real answer is to feel.'

THE TRUTH ABOUT MANIFESTING

'What your mind can dream, your hands can achieve.'

When I first heard about manifesting. I thought it meant just thinking about what I wanted, and then, poof! A magic fairy would show up to grant all my wishes. No effort needed. Back then, I only tried to manifest 'things' because I thought that's what manifesting was all about. If you've ever felt this way, I get it! In this chapter, I'll reveal the reality behind manifesting and what it truly takes to bring your desires to life.

Manifestation is a particularly popular subject at this time. I want to set the record straight on the practice, as I believe many teachers, mentors, and coaches have made what should be a straightforward tool overly complicated and confusing.

When we think happy thoughts, more happy things will come our way; when we think unhappy thoughts, more unhappy things will come to us. This is the simplest way I've come up with to define manifestation. Of course, there's a lot more to the subject, but it covers the basics.

We are made up of energy, and we also emit energy. This explains why you can sometimes sense when someone is feeling sad, distressed or happy without them saying a word. Our job here on earth is to manipulate our energy. This may sound complex, but really, it boils down to simply understanding that you are powerful and can have whatever you wish for. There are a few things that prevent people from realising the power of manifestation, but the main issue is a lack of knowledge of the practices involved and the tools at their disposal, a lack of belief in their own ability, and an unclear idea about what they want from life.

I have a trick that will make the whole process straightforward.

Some teachers will tell you, "All you have to do is think about what you want. Journal and meditate on it, and you will receive it." I am not saying they're wrong to say this, but attempting manifestation in this way didn't work for me; if anything, it made me ungrateful for what I had, frustrated about what I wanted, and very materialistic overall. Now, there's no shame in wanting nice things; we all want a great life! But I hadn't been that way before I tried manifesting. I started caring way more about money than the impact and love I gave to the world. My moment of clarity came when I realised that:

'Manifestation isn't about what you GET, but what you GIVE.'

Once I'd found this missing key, I began to focus on enjoying life, trusting the process, living in the moment and making choices that made me happy, and it worked! I'd been so focused on the outcome that I missed YEARS of my life. I do not want you to make the same mistake, but even if you've spent a long time on the wrong path, I can assure you it's never too late to make a comeback.

Many people misinterpret the information that manifesting teachers, coaches, and gurus say. Some wait for the 'magic' to hit them in the face one day, but the truth is, we make the magic.

We make choices that turn our lives into pure magic.

We are the magic.

Remember, our words and thoughts create energy, so remember to check in with yourself to see if your thoughts are aligned with who you truly are and who you want to be.

There is another key aspect that I don't hear or read many spiritual teachers teaching.

Action…

Before learning about the action part of manifesting, I genuinely thought if I wrote my aspirations down, manifested them every day and sat and waited, they would come to me without taking any action and following through with new ideas. I thought that if I was wishful thinking every day but making no change to my life, a little pixie would come out of a mushroom and hand me everything I wanted... okay, that's not exactly what I thought, but you get the gist! That may work somewhere in another universe with goblins and little magical creatures floating around, but in my experience, that is not how it happened to me.

Let's say you manifest something; the more you think about it, the more related things will reveal themselves, and new thoughts and perspectives will come to you. This is how our minds work; the mind always tries to confirm whatever we choose to believe.

If you want to manifest a new job but are not looking online or handing out your CV, and you're not even going out, how on earth will you find a new job? Something may crop up out of the blue; things like that do happen, but I'm pointing out that manifestation still requires action from you.

What frequency do you emit?

Think about what state of being you are in most of the day. Are you often sad, angry, stressed, and pessimistic, or are you generally upbeat, grateful for what you have, calm, optimistic and taking things as they come? The

energy we emit into the world attracts the same energy through people, objects, events, and situations.
Don't beat yourself up about what frequency you have been emitting; become aware of it.

It's important to follow the path of least resistance to manifest effectively and work in a way that aligns with you. But what does "the path of least resistance" mean? Resistance itself isn't a bad thing; think about exercise resistance, which builds muscle. A little resistance can help us grow, push through challenges, and reach the next stage in our personal development, work, or goals. But too much resistance? That's a recipe for burnout, being overwhelmed, or breaking point, especially for those of us who are wired differently, like someone with dyslexia or other neurodivergent traits.

Following the path of least resistance means finding *your* way of doing things and finding 'your' flow that works best for you. It's about recognising that there are often easier, less stressful ways to achieve your goals if you stop trying to force yourself into methods that don't suit you.

Some people thrive with high resistance and intense challenges, which drives them. Others prefer a gentler approach that allows for more flexibility and creativity. Neither is right or wrong; it's about what works best for you. Your journey is yours alone. Honour your uniqueness and create systems, routines, and habits that support your growth without unnecessary struggle. The key is finding what keeps you moving forward without burning yourself out in the process.

Guide to Manifesting:

1. Be consistent

Rome was not built in a day, and neither will your manifestation. You can't do one self-development exercise and instantly transform your mindset to a state where you naturally think empowering and positive thoughts. This takes repetition; research shows that it can take learning a piece of information 7-20 times before it fully sinks into the subconscious.

2. Feel it

You must feel the feeling. Let's say you want to be a big movie star: you must *feel* like one before becoming that star. Or, if your manifestation is to have a supporting and loving partner, yes, that's right; you've got to feel it, not just think about it. This is because emotions amplify your intentions and align your subconscious mind with your desires.

3. Enjoy the journey of life

This means embracing the present moment and finding fulfilment, joy, and growth in the process of living rather than fixating solely on future goals or outcomes. It's about appreciating where you are, who you are becoming, and what you are experiencing right now rather than constantly focusing on what's next.

4. Take action!
You can manifest as much as you like, but without action, nothing will happen. Think, feel, and act, which are critical components of manifesting your desires. The action bridges the gap between your vision and reality.

I believe it's important to feel that you already have what you desire, but the easiest way to do so is to enjoy what you are doing and be present. Once you know what you want, the aim is to come back to that feeling of already having it as many times as possible. Let me say that again.

'The Aim Is To Come Back To That Feeling Of Already Having It As Many Times As You Can.'

I hear a lot of teachings and tools in the manifesting space about knowing exactly what you want, every detail, every aspect. Yes, have an idea of what you want for your life, but every detail? I tried this, and it didn't work for me. It left me feeling confused, frustrated and, quite frankly, pissed off.

I would only like you to refrain from this if that way of manifesting isn't working for you because trying to control every aspect of life pushes us away from the best thing for us. If you have found another way that works better for you, stick with what you know and what works. If we say, 'I want this car' or 'this exact house,' it limits what we could have. What if there is a better house or life beyond your wildest dreams? This doesn't allow life to flow and limits you to what is 'best' for you. Remember, there is no right or wrong; I say, try it all and see what feels best suited for you.

Of course, know what kind of life you want: purposeful, fulfilling, successful, driven, peaceful or happy, but try not to limit yourself to every detail. Allow life to flow, and you will find things gravitate more toward you when you *let go*. This was a hard concept for me to grasp, but you know what I found? When I surrendered and stopped trying to control my future and let myself be guided freely… I felt lighter, free, guided, and reassured. I opened every door. If they didn't feel right, I would close them and keep all my options and paths clear.

In my self-development journey, I have found that many tools and practices contradict themselves. Still, I promise to let go and have every bit of trust in your higher self, god, the universe, or Mother Nature, whoever you feel like calling upon.

Let's say, one day, you want to manifest one path in life, and then a week or two goes by, and now, you've changed your mind about what path you want to take. It's fine; these things happen. Personally, I was terrible at this. I couldn't fully make up my mind about what I wanted externally, material objects like cars, houses, laptops, or clothes to manifest. When this happens, we create a block for our manifestations to manifest, as the universe, god, Mother Nature, or higher self now doesn't know what you want. This means your energy is shifting and changing too frequently for energy to match. This is exactly what happened to me. We grow, adapt, and evolve and are meant to change.

A few years ago, I went to a spiritual development workshop. Jane Goodman was our mentor, who now isn't just a teacher; she's a friend. She is renowned for her spiritual wisdom, and I learned much from her. During one workshop session, she said something to me that would change the course of my life. She asked me...
"Instead of manifesting external things, items, cars, jobs and houses, if you are not 100% sure what you want, how about manifesting a feeling?"

Have you ever experienced a light-bulb moment? That instant when one piece of information makes everything else make sense and become clearer? I had that moment. Instead of manifesting material things, the key is manifesting the feeling.

When we cultivate a certain feeling, material things naturally follow. Manifesting a feeling brings more benefits than just acquiring items. After all, we often seek material things to achieve a particular feeling. By focusing on manifesting the feeling itself, we can achieve a deeper, more lasting fulfilment.

It's essential to understand that practising gratitude can significantly benefit you in various aspects of your life. When you're striving to achieve success in any area of your life, it's important to immerse yourself in the emotions and mindset of already being successful. It's also crucial to express deep gratitude for all the blessings and opportunities you currently have in your life. By embracing gratitude and visualising success, we can all create a powerful and positive mindset that propels us toward our goals.

'Some people wait for the 'magic' to hit them in the face one day, but the truth is we make the magic; we make choices that turn our lives into pure magic.'

MANIFESTING WITHOUT VIBRATION IS POINTLESS

'Manifesting without feeling it is like planting a seed and never watering it.'
- Unknown

After years of studying the law of attraction and reading every book I could find, it finally came to me. Just because you read all the books, write down your gratitude every morning, practise manifesting and meditations, count your blessings, and hold your crystals, that doesn't mean you are on the same frequency as what you want from life. You must feel it.

The word 'vibe' is used so much in conversation these days, but for a long time, I only understood the word's general meaning. Every morning for years, I would do a *Magic Morning* (something I will touch base on in another chapter). I would write out 3-10 things I was grateful for and do a 5-8 minute half-hearted meditation while still thinking of work and what messages I 'needed' to reply to. I would write affirmation after affirmation, hoping these 'magic' steps would lead me to happiness, fortune and luck.

Guess what? It didn't work. After years and years, I was still overworking, just breaking even, stressed, overstimulated and just damn right confused at that point. How strange... I followed all the steps in all the books I'd read and the courses I'd taken. What was missing?

THE VIBE.

The term 'vibe' refers to the **emotional atmosphere** or **energy** that a person, place, or situation gives off, which can influence how you feel when you're around it. When people say "feel the vibe," they mean to tune into the environment or person's underlying mood, energy, or emotional tone. It's about sensing the **emotional frequency** or **state of being** that surrounds you or that someone is projecting and then reacting to it emotionally.

So when you fail to feel it, you fail to hold it.

I didn't truly connect with what I was affirming. I just went through the motions, saying my affirmations and writing them down, then rushing through my day in a frantic state of: *'I MUST HAVE MORE.'* But here's the thing: if you don't put the energy into truly feeling your affirmations and feeling them with every cell in your body, you'll end up wasting time, feeling drained, and prolonging your situation. As I've said before, it's about choosing the path of least resistance that works best for YOU as an individual.

In university, I was infatuated with the human brain and the frequency at which we vibrate. If you haven't seen music create a pattern, you must stop what you are doing now and YouTube "Cymatics: Chladni Plate - Sound, Vibration and Sand". It's incredible! This is the actual proof that the sounds and words we say create different vibrations that affect us.

We can sometimes lie to ourselves; I know I have for years. I was under the hard stress of what we call 'The rat race', which was draining, lonely and unenjoyable. I wanted to be financially free, and I thought opening a business in a popular industry was the best thing to do. But something didn't **feel** right; the more money that came in, the more money went out. I had read so many books about money and financial freedom, and I was doing everything the books said to do. I didn't understand why I had invested a great deal of money into my businesses but was getting nothing in return, but what was missing... the vibe. I thought to get what I desired, I had to vibrate at the same energy level as the thing I wanted. As much as this seems right, and many people teach this method and theory, something was still missing; something didn't **feel** right.

I was what people call 'selling my soul' for money.
I'm all about animal rights, natural beauty, and self-love, yet I worked in the beauty and aesthetics industry that tested on animals, despite the money I donated to animal charities to stop the testing. What I was doing was completely out of my morals, beliefs, and values.
I started to realise that it didn't matter how much I tried to jump on the energy level; it didn't vibrate on my frequency!

So the question is, what did I do?

LET GO of my morals and what I truly believed in (which was never going to happen), or LET GO of the business that wasn't serving me or aligned with me?

 I wasn't vibrating on the same wave as that industry, as we all admit a unique frequency. I wasn't making any changes to my life. All I was doing was lying to myself and burying my head under the sand. The universe/god/Mother Nature took the reins and pushed me out of my workspace, forcing me to listen to myself and believe deep down that I know what is right for me.

Years of work equipment took over my small home, and the planning permission to build a new workspace in my garden was denied. What did I do? Cry? No. Get stressed? Maybe a little, but hardly. I let go... let go of every idea of what I was going to do with my life and my business. I even let go of the idea of having a business. I just let the f*ck go, and you know what... it felt AMAZING! I felt liberated for the first time. It wasn't then that I realised my true calling: to help people and animals.

I wish I could tell you I listened to my higher self, connected all the obvious dots, and gracefully shut down my businesses. But the universe had bigger plans for me. I didn't listen, so life stepped in and made things harder, not just to shake me out of it but to ensure I learned the deeper lessons I had been avoiding.

The universe, your higher self, God, or Mother Nature, whatever you resonate with, will always give you what is truly meant for you, whether it feels positive or negative in the moment. Life's challenges and blessings come to you because they're aligned with what you can handle and what will help you grow. But here's the catch: it's not enough to simply dream or wish. You must show you're ready by backing up your words with action. Manifestation isn't magic; it's a partnership between your intentions and effort.

When you take action on what you want, you're proving to yourself and the universe that you're serious about creating the life you desire. So don't just speak your dreams into existence. Live them into reality. Every step forward is a message to the universe.

Get your notepad and pen ready for this one; it's time to get real with yourself.

Write down your answer to this question, and take as long as you need. If you can't answer it right away, that's okay. Come back to it when you're ready.

Is there anything you're hiding from yourself?
Be honest with yourself. This isn't about judgment or pressure but about gaining clarity. Sometimes, we convince ourselves that we're on the right path because it feels easier or safer than facing the truth.

THE POWER OF DEFAULT ENERGY

'Default energy is like a river flowing in a certain direction. It takes conscious effort to change its course, but once you do, the possibilities become endless.'

When I began to explore the idea of default energy, I couldn't help but think back to my childhood and the energy in and around my family. My dad was in the 7th Parachute Regiment RHA, serving in the military, a career that demanded resilience and discipline. But everything in his world (and ours) changed in a split second.

During a jump, he leapt from 700 feet into gusting winds, which sent him hurtling through the air before slamming into the ground. The injuries he sustained were so severe that the hospital nearly amputated his foot.

That one moment didn't just change his life. It shifted the energy in our home. Looking back, it's clear how moments like that shape the way we show up in the world, whether we're conscious of it or not.

As a sergeant, he was used to keeping everyone in line, so you can imagine the strict, intense energy that filled our home. When his accident happened, everything he'd known since he was 18 was torn away. He was frustrated, angry, and grieving the life he'd lost, not to mention the trauma he'd faced as a child himself.

My dad, mum, and nan were all struggling with depression. My mum found it hard to manage when my dad was suddenly home all the time, and vice versa. Even though my brother and I were loved, the household energy was heavy and low, suffocating in many ways. This type of energy can have a huge impact on children, shaping them as they grow. That's exactly what I started to uncover as I learned about the power of default energy.

Our minds are incredibly powerful, yet we only tap into a fraction of their full potential. While the mind is always working to protect us, this instinct can sometimes do more harm than good, even though it has the best intentions.

I'm going to use myself as an example here: I used to be a very sad, depressed, and angry person. As I mentioned before, I was hitting rock bottom every day due to my upbringing being in a strained and angry environment. It's not like my upbringing was 'bad', but the energy of the household affected my daily life. My mind became accustomed to being sad, so it became comfortable... and because that was my default state, my mind processed sadness and anger as a 'safe place' for me.

Let me say that again: the environment I was brought up in, surrounded by people who were unhappy, stuck, and argumentative, directly influenced my 'default energy.' Being around that lower vibrational frequency shaped how I saw the world and how I showed up in it.

The simplest example would be that the happy or sad environment you were brought up in has created your natural default energy, so if you were brought up in an unhappy, suppressed, or angry house, the chances are that sadness will be comforting to you somehow. The first time you admit that to yourself can be pretty challenging, but realising it is the first step to change.

We can change our default energy by not only becoming aware of it but also learning more about ourselves, like what the little voice inside of our head says. Becoming aware of this helps you to hear if the little voice is saying disempowering statements, like "I'm not good enough", "I will always feel this way", or "I am broken". These negative statements hold an energy\vibe\frequency which affects your mood. When you have recognised these unhelpful statements, your little voice keeps repeating; it's your job to flip them to more empowering statements like "I am good enough" or "I have the ability, power and choice to change".

The only person who can truly help you is yourself; when you realise that you have a choice in what thoughts you listen to, it is extremely powerful in itself. Even though it's easier said than done, it takes consistency and committed action from yourself to do the self-development work. A great tip is to write down your limited statements like "I'm never going to do it", so you can see exactly what your internal voice is saying; this may make it easier to flip them, in this case, from "I'm never going to do it" to "I'm going to do it with time and practice".

Now I look back at that time in my life, I can admit it... I liked being sad! The comfort I found in being unhappy came from the power of default energy.

Don't get me wrong; some of these traits are woven into our DNA. I learned this while studying for my Level 2 mental health exams. If a mother is constantly stressed, depressed, dealing with trauma, or experiencing high levels of inflammation, that gets passed on. It's been passed on to me, too, but I don't let it take over or consume me anymore. I've come to understand that I have more control over my life than I ever thought possible.

Breaking free from your default energy might seem simple; all you have to do is re-program your mind. But not quite. Our minds love staying in their little protected bubble box to make our lives easier and less stressful. Can you see how our minds can contradict themselves? They keep us safe by keeping us in our default comfortable energy, but if our natural state of default is negative and disempowering, if anything, it's our own minds keeping us from being happy, positive and empowered.

The question is, after we have learned more about ourselves, become aware of that little voice and switch these negative statements to more empowering ones, how do we maintain a high energy?

CONSISTENCY!

When you feel or think in a 'negative' or non-supportive way, change the energy immediately and try not to let your mind dwell or stay in your 'non-helpful', 'default energy'. You must be consistent with this practice; as I said before, Rome was not built in a day. You do not get bigger muscles after one gym session; just like this, you cannot simply change your embedded default energy after practising this once.

One of the best ways to snap yourself out of these low moods is to use this 'magic trick' that most people know but little use…

GRATITUDE. Simple, huh?

 Yes, actually, it is!
 I remember when I physically couldn't think of anything to be grateful for, but now I sit back and think, 'How selfish!'

Here we are with air to breathe, water to drink, and shelter to keep ourselves warm and dry, oh yeh and another day to be alive! It can be easy to be grateful for the above, but what about being grateful for your body parts?

Your heart beats for YOU all day, keeping you alive.
Your veins carry blood throughout your body.
Your lungs allow you to breathe oxygen into your body.
Your brain is helping you read or listen to this book and mentally function.

If you are lucky enough to have a warm bed tonight, get in, close your eyes and be grateful you are warm and safe. This is an excellent start to becoming aware of the thing you are genuinely grateful for. This may seem pointless to someone new on this journey, but I will tell you a fact that will stick with you for your lifetime.

'Gratitude is the highest frequency level.'

All you need to do is pick a few things you are genuinely grateful for, FEEL them, and your mood and energy will 100% change. Now, that is science.

Being sad is an addiction, not for all people but for some; the truth is that your default energy is set to a certain emotional state. This emotional state starts to become our comfort. Many people's 'down days' are right in their comfort zones, which means they want to feel more of it as our mind wants to keep us comfortable. The more down days you have, not only will you be staying in your comfort zone, but you will also be stuck in a loop of sadness.

Let's say you've noticed that you are feeling unhappy and low. You start to get on a more positive energy level. One day you feel a little crap, and decide to have a day off from being positive and grateful, then you start feeling sorry for yourself and curl up on the sofa. That day then turns into a couple of days that turn into a week, then a month, etc., because being sad can become an addiction, a craving for comfort.

I know this because I, too, was stuck in this depressive loop for years on end. Our whole lives are based around loops, disempowering loops and empowering loops. In this book, I will not only show you how they work and how to retrain them but also teach you the knowledge behind WHY; this will help you not only retrain your mind, thought process, and energy but also create long-lasting change!

It's okay to admit you have been addicted to or like the sadness and self-pity I've been there. I can openly say I LOVED being sad, but after I learned everything I am about to teach you and have already taught you, holding onto sadness no longer made sense. When you have the same perspective on life as I now have, wasting another minute on any low mood literally doesn't make any sense, and I can't wait to unravel everything I know and help you in a beautiful, profound way!

Get your notepad and pen and ask yourself these questions:

 1. Does being sad make me feel comfortable and weirdly happy?
2. If yes, what happened in my life to make being sad comfortable for me?
3. What are the consequences if I do not change my self-talk to a more empowering one?
4. When I next hear my little voice speak negatively, what actions will I take?
5. Why is it important for me to start becoming aware and flipping my internal voice?

WE GET TO CHOOSE OUR PATH

'Choosing your path isn't about perfection; it's about progress in the direction that feels right to you.'

Before I fully embraced the idea that we could choose our path, I felt trapped, like I was just being pulled along with no say in where I was headed. Growing up with the experiences I had, I convinced myself that happiness was reserved for other people and that I couldn't access the tools to help my mindset grow. I felt like life was happening *to* me, not *for* me, while my mind ran on a loop of negative thoughts, spiralling around in disempowering circles that left me feeling stuck and small.

Then came a realisation that shook me to my core: I do have a choice! I could choose learning over stagnation, growth over just 'getting by, ' and change over staying in my comfort zone. I could break free from those old beliefs and step into a completely new way of being. Once I saw that freedom, life began to open up in ways I never imagined. I could choose to heal, to grow, to design my life. And let me tell you, when you get to that point, life becomes a whole new adventure, one that you shape with every choice.

This is a really exciting chapter because life gets better when you realise this is the truth. It's okay if this doesn't immediately impact your life or sink in, but let's plant that seed.

We get to make our own way in life. There is no 'one path that fits all' because we are so incredibly different. Success and happiness are different for each individual, and we get to make this choice. It's important to understand that down days and sad moments are a part of the journey.

Without rain, plants wouldn't grow.

We need to have pain and f*ck ups to help us grow and learn and make sure to be grateful for all the mistakes and the pain we have been through instead of dwelling and playing the victim.

Think about it for a moment. *What have you learned from those situations?*

We are living beings having human experiences. Some of those human experiences aren't great, and some leave us stuck in a rut. This is normal, but sometimes, we choose to stay in those ruts for days, weeks, and years. Sometimes, we do this because we believe escape is beyond our control. However . . .

WE GET TO CHOOSE TO BE happy. I can speak about this from experience. I once thought I had no control over my thoughts, emotions and energy, and I truly believed that it was simply the way my brain worked. You might feel that way now. You may be telling yourself you'll never be able to change that. This is not true. You have been conditioned to feel this way through no fault of your own.

WE GET TO CHOOSE to shift our energy. Whenever a negative or unhelpful thought comes your way, acknowledge it, move on and let it go. Why? Because life can be too short. I know. I have lost people and animals that were too young to pass, too young to have their whole lives taken away. Hold that thought and be grateful for your life. Live every moment, feel every moment and make choices that will make you happy.

'Let go and allow everything to flow.'

WE GET TO CHOOSE what thoughts to expand on and what ones to ignore. We are HUMAN! We can think silly thoughts, and just because you think a questionable, weird thought sometimes does not mean you are weird; it just means you had a thought... that's it! Sometimes, a horrible thought about someone comes to your mind: What do you do? Choose to expand on it, or know you are not that kind of person and move on? Whenever you think of a negative or self-destructive thought, as soon as you realise what you are doing, switch it to one that aligns with the person you want to be or are deep down.

I hope you understand the magic in this: YOU HAVE A CHOICE! I get what it's like to have the most horrific thoughts and to feel like you have no choice, but you do, and your choices will determine your outcomes in life.

Let me say that again.

'YOUR CHOICES DETERMINE YOUR OUTCOMES IN LIFE'

Limited beliefs can show up in so many ways, and one of the most common is believing that *we can't control how we feel.* I held onto this belief for years, making excuses for the negative thoughts and feelings that kept flooding my mind. It consumed me and prolonged my ideas, leaving me stuck. That's why it's so important to know this: *you have a choice.* It doesn't mean blocking out every 'bad' or self-doubting thought; they're part of being human. Instead, feel them, hear them, and then take action to shift them into something empowering. It's not always easy, but it's possible, and it takes consistency... a lot of it.

So, what do you want? What do you choose?

Grab your notepad and pen, and answer these questions:
1. What does my ideal day look like from start to finish?

2. What thoughts or beliefs are holding me back from living the life I want?
3. How do I want to show up for myself and others every day?
4. What habits or routines would support the emotions and experiences I want to create?
5. What does success look and feel like to me personally?

Get crystal clear on what you want to improve in your life. And remember: You *always* have the choice to take that first step toward the life you truly desire. It's not impossible; it might even be easier than you think.

The goal? Keep going. Keep choosing. And create a life that aligns with the future *you* want.

FOLLOW THE PATH OF LESS RESISTANCE

Choosing the path of least resistance reduces stress, aligns you with your natural flow, and saves energy for what truly matters. It allows for clarity, personal growth, and flexibility while fostering trust in the process of life. Rather than constantly fighting against circumstances, you embrace a more harmonious way of living, leading to greater peace and fulfilment. This is where 'let go and allow everything to flow' comes from.

By that, I do not mean sitting on the sofa watching rubbish TV or allowing yourself to be consumed with self-destructive habits. You may feel like that occasionally when you've had a hard day and need time to switch off, but what I mean is to take some time and space to see and feel what you really, deep down, want to do/act and be.

You can have or do anything you want; it's not about knowing how; it's about knowing why. You just need to choose to believe in yourself and your own abilities. It might sound cliché, but honestly, clichés are often the simplest, most effective advice.

That's why it's important to FOLLOW THE PATH OF LESS RESISTANCE to make it easier for you. I choose not to push myself to the edge. I'm not saying this isn't a great way to achieve success, but I was not built for that. I am a neurodivergent human, and acting in that way, not leaving creative space and switching off time, leads me to burn out. I've learned that through my last business. It made me very ill; now, I allow myself to do as much as I feel like doing and then have a break before getting right back to it. Following the path of least resistance is individual, and only you can measure what works for you.

That seed will grow into a plant, and you will find your way. You get to choose the stories you are telling yourself about yourself.

I've always been on the lazy side as a child, and that carried with me throughout my adult life; you know why? When I was a child, I was constantly told I was lazy. In the back of my head, I would hear, 'You know you're not going to finish that because you are lazy' or 'I know I'm lazy, so I'm going to leave the house a sh*t state…

What stories are you holding on to about yourself?

Get your notepad and pen and write that question. Take as long as you need to answer it. Maybe it's a small story like mine about being lazy, or maybe it's a bad situation you have been through, and instead of healing and moving on, it's become an unhealthy part of you and your story.

The reason I ask you to do this is because the stories and statements that we say and hear on repeat create our reality. It's all about catching yourself before you fall down a self-destructive road.

Maybe your parents, an ex or a teacher had told you something, and now it's stuck. The thing is, I don't believe in punishing your parents or old teachers; try not to be too hard on them. We are all humans and make mistakes, and I would never punish my parents for implanting certain things and stories in my head because they didn't have this knowledge. These people lived in a much more difficult time compared to us, in a time when mental health didn't exist; when people were so poor, they shared a bed with all their siblings and would only get the food they were given. Be kind to people, and when you're on your self-help/healing journey, maybe you can help some of those people along the way.

'The path of least resistance isn't about taking the easy way out; it's about aligning with what feels right and letting life unfold naturally.'

'Tomorrow does not belong to us.'

TOMORROW IS NOT PROMISED

'Yesterday is history, tomorrow is a mystery, today is a gift. That's why we call it the present.'

- Eleanor Roosevelt

My life changed dramatically when I started to lose the people and things I loved around me. This is when I embodied this simple fact that 'tomorrow is not promised'.

WARNING: Sensitive information.
Please be aware that this chapter contains triggering stories and information. I could have only written about the fluffy things in life, all about how amazing our minds are and how magical the world is. However, context like this is still very important. Death is a part of life, and it's something we should not run away from. I truly believe this is an eye-opening, life-changing chapter. Some of the toughest and most painful lessons in life are the ones that trigger a wake-up call.

In this chapter, I explain the pain of not wanting to be on this earth anymore and the pain and hardship of losing loved ones. What is in this chapter helped me realise how precious, short and magical life can really be. But I'd just like to warn readers before I jump in.

I would like you to know that I completely understand what it feels like not to want to be here anymore. It's a sad, lonely, confusing place, but I promise the information in this book will help you, and it will get easier. I know what it's like to feel that the whole world is pointless.

The thing is, life can be pointless, and here's why: 'The only point to life is the point you give it.'

Let's return to the last chapters; what do you choose? To live a life with no meaning, no point, and be unhappy, unmotivated, and sad? Or find a point and meaning to life?

Because, as you now know, you have the choice.

Do you know why so many people are unhappy? Because it's easy... yes, I said it, IT'S EASY!

Working through trauma, learning new coping mechanisms, changing your lifestyle, and perceiving life in a positive light takes consistency, and consistency takes practice and hard work.

Most people, when they are young, don't realise how fragile and remarkable our bodies and our lives are. When I was in university, it was somewhat 'popular' to be depressed; even worse, it was 'trending' to hurt yourself at school. This was difficult for the people who were actually suffering childhood trauma; I personally never spoke about how I felt to anyone. I didn't want people to think I was attention-seeking like some of my peers. But I now know it's incredibly important to reach out for help; if you are struggling, know that you are not alone and that there are so many resources online which were not around back then.

I can't emphasise this enough: it is not cool, trendy, or fun to hurt yourself or to feel sad or depressed. Doing so drains your energy and steals your life, taking away the real you. It erases your true character and personality, leaving you feeling lost, lonely, confused, and sad.

If you have lost someone or something you loved, you will understand how painful this really is. I've lost aunties and uncles, but nothing compares to the pain of losing my kitten. She was run over and left for dead for six days before someone found her. Peaches was my little fur baby. We have two Maine Coon cats, Crystal and Baloo, and they had 6 beautiful kittens; we kept two, Yoshi and Peaches.

Grief is indescribable, an experience so unique to each individual that there is no 'right' or 'wrong' way to grieve. The best advice is often no advice at all. No matter how much someone tries to help with words, nothing can take away the pain. Grief is something we must all come to terms with in our own time, in our own way. As I write this, I admit I still struggle to fully grasp the reality of losing her.

But if there's one thing I've learned after her death, it's the simple fact that tomorrow is not promised. Losing Peaches was the beginning of a wake-up call!

After Peaches died, I started to understand and feel that there is no point in feeling sad and frustrated about the things we can't control.

Don't get me wrong, that is not how I felt the first year or two; losing someone or something is no joke. Do you know what hit me the most? The guilt I felt because of how many times I used to wish my life away; how come I could live a perfectly healthy, beautiful life and want to give that all up when there are innocent souls who want to live?

I'm not here to shame you for your past; **you are not obligated to be the person you were *two months, two weeks, or even two days ago.*** Every morning you wake up, you can choose what person you are and what actions you take. I am here to help you, guide you, and open your eyes and mind to a life where you can create anything you want, including happiness and peace. Realising this, becoming aware of it, and remembering it will help.

While I was writing this book, one of my aunties suddenly passed away. Not only was she an Auntie, she was a friend. She was fit and healthy and went to the gym every morning at 5:30 am. She was always well dressed and presented, beautiful, kind, loving and pure... I could go on for hours. The thing is, one day, out of nowhere, with no warning, she just passed away.

Something similar may have happened to you. If this hasn't happened to you, I would like you to take a moment and think about someone you love. Seeing them one day, fit, healthy, happy, then never to see them again.

The day after losing her, the pieces of my business I was holding onto, I finally decided to let go. I sold my equipment and handed in the lease to my salon.

Do you know why?

Because tomorrow isn't promised, I realised that I no longer wanted to spend time on anything that didn't bring me happiness or align with who I truly am. That's when this book, which started as a personal journal on how I navigate life and business with dyslexia, evolved into the self-help book you are reading now. I became certified as a life coach and launched *Thrive Beyond Limits*, my online mindset coaching platform. I knew I wanted to step away from the beauty industry, where the focus was on physical appearances, and instead help people on a much deeper, spiritual level.

This is why I live by this statement: *TOMORROW IS NOT PROMISED.*

I started to wake up to the fact that most of us spend our precious time here overthinking, worrying, fearful and full of self-doubt.

Let's let that information fully sink in because our lives are so temporary, too temporary, to hold onto past pain and allow it to consume our every day. Death is very strange and confusing for all people as we don't know what happens when it's all over, and for all we know, we get one shot to live, so why not live it in the way you truly want to?

Why not be happy? Why stress? Why get angry? Why get frustrated?

I'm not saying you should avoid feeling anything, but it's important to be consciously aware of the thoughts we are letting in. By reevaluating whether you want these thoughts in your mind, you can start to eliminate the made-up problems we often create for ourselves.

There was this video that went viral on social media, where Eddie Murphy said, 'If you live 75 years, you get 75 summers, 75 winters, 75 birthdays, and 75 Christmases. Why waste our very precious time focusing on negative things? His point was that when we put it into perspective, our time here is short; don't waste your energy and time on things we cannot control.

Look, I get it; life can be unfortunate. Let's think about it in depth: we are all going to pass away at some point, and we are all going to have heartbreak and physical pain in our lives. Instead of freaking out, accept it, embrace it because you know what starts to happen? Life gets magical. Acknowledging that this life is not forever puts things and life itself into perspective. This is life, and stressing or getting sad about most situations will not change the outcome; the goal is to remain calm and at peace while still accepting, feeling and acknowledging the pain, hurt and emotions.

That said, it is important to feel positive feelings and negative feelings instead of suppressing these emotions. Nothing, and I mean nothing, will make you feel better about losing someone or something, especially when that someone or something is too young to pass. If, like me, you have had this tragic experience of loved ones ending their life or having their life cut short by another being, it's normal to feel guilt, anger, and resentment. Even though it can be difficult, feeling this pain will help you; blocking it will only cause damage to yourself. It's the yin with the yang.

LATER IS NOT OURS TO SAVE

We often say, "I'll do it later", "I'll call them later," and "I'll do that tomorrow", but 'later' doesn't belong to us, and it's not ours to save because of the fact that tomorrow is not promised. I'm not here to scare you; I'm here to bring your awareness to the inevitable: we die. All of us. Being scared of it isn't going to stop it from happening one day. When you are not fully living in the moment, this tends to make the journey of life go faster.

I love life

Say it out loud. Do you know why? Because it can be short, love it. Feel the love with every cell in your body; love, accept, feel. I can't express it enough: just be grateful for this and every moment, be thankful for family, spend more time with the people you love, respect, and accept them. Because one day, they will be a memory. I know it can be unpleasant to think this way, but it makes us remember what is truly important in life and why we choose happiness over anything else.

Do you really want to be lying on your deathbed thinking, 'I wish I had been more outgoing; I wish I hadn't cared as much; I wish I had done more of what made me happy and stopped overthinking everything; I wish I had lived in the moment, and not in my head?

Here's an activity for you: Write one of these statements, pick one that resonates with you, or make one up with the same meaning and put it somewhere you look at every day, like near the kettle, on the mirror in your car. Write it down every day! Start to live and breathe it because when you do, you won't miss your life while it flashes before your eyes.

'Live every moment with every cell in my body.'
'Live life like tomorrow isn't guaranteed.'
'Tomorrow isn't promised.'
'Be fully alive in every breath you take.'
'Make today count; it's the only one guaranteed.'
'Live like the moment you're in is the only one that matters.'
'Don't save your best for later; give it everything now.'
'Life happens now, so don't miss it.'
'Own every second like it's borrowed time.'
'The future is uncertain, but this moment is yours.'

HOW TO LET THE F*CK GO

'Holding on is more painful than letting go, it gives your rope burn. Let go and allow everything to flow'

For years, I was living in a story, a story rooted in my past. I held onto the pain, the trauma, and the narratives that I thought defined me. These stories weren't just memories; they became woven into my identity so deeply that breaking free felt almost impossible. Without even realising it, I'd fused these experiences with who I was. Letting go wasn't a quick process, but it was one of the most liberating things I've ever done.

In this chapter, I hope to share the knowledge, tools, and strength that helped me finally detach from those old stories and step into the present. We all have the power to release what no longer serves us, to leave behind what weighs us down, and to live fully, right here, right now.

'Let this be the moment you choose to let go and reclaim yourself.'

As you now know, life is too short, magical and precious to hold onto the past events that have happened; it's very easy to stay and hold on for life as it is our natural conditioning; these events, though painful, make us feel comfortable, which leads us to hold on to them, even though they no longer serve us.

Holding on is natural, but letting go is a choice; our human minds are hard-wired for survival, which means that when an event happens in our lives, our minds are designed to hold on to it just in case it happens again to protect ourselves. As we know from 'the power of default energy', our mind keeps us safe, but it contradicts itself.

The thing is, keeping us 'safe' and following our instincts may lead to mental pain and suffering. Now, I don't mean intuition. Intuition is the inner knowing, the gut feeling that nudges you towards what feels right, whereas instincts are the fight-or-flight hard-wired conditioning.

Here's an example: You went through a painful breakup. Your mind holds on to that hurt as a way to protect you, building walls to keep you from getting hurt again. So now, anytime a new relationship arises, you might instinctively shut down or push people away.

It feels like staying "safe," but really, it's keeping you stuck in pain. That instinct to protect yourself ends up causing more suffering, which isolates you, keeps you from feeling love and makes it hard to open up. The mind's attempt to protect you is actually doing the opposite, creating mental and emotional pain by holding you back from the happiness and connection you could have. By doing this, you're not allowing yourself to let go of what no longer serves you.

In some cases, the event, person, or emotions become so embedded in us that the story becomes our identity; this happens especially when it's a traumatic event. When we make the story our identity, whether unconsciously or consciously, it becomes very hard to let go, and it can feel like we are losing or letting go of part of ourselves.

You are normal, this is normal, and it's just the mind trying to protect us. We understand that this is counterproductive. Letting go takes time and consistency; I coach people daily on letting go, but first, you must give yourself permission to let go and forgive yourself for holding onto it.

Ask yourself, *How is holding on benefiting me?*

Because often, holding on hurts far more than letting go. Clinging to painful stories and events is like gripping a rope too tightly. It burns your hands, causing more and more pain. The longer you hold on, the worse it gets. Our mind's 'safety mechanism' tells us to hang on for dear life, as if letting go would drop us into a shark tank. But in reality, this is just the mind's way of trying to protect us. The truth is, when we let go, the pain begins to ease. It may not happen instantly, but releasing bit by bit allows us to lighten our load, let go of the baggage, and finally move forward.

We as humans hold onto other things like control; I spoke about it briefly earlier. We can't control the outcome, how we will achieve our goal, and other people's journeys, opinions and lives. Once we LET THE F*CK GO, oh my... life starts to flow in such a beautiful way!

When you are ready to take the step to let go, I'd like you to try this:

Step 1: Close your eyes, get comfortable, take three deep breaths, and start becoming aware of an event, person or story that is holding you back that you just can't shake off. Now feel the weight of that story, person or event, feel it physically holding you down, and start to notice the heaviness in your body. Maybe you are feeling low or pressure, even weight on your shoulders. It's important to feel this physically.

Step 2: Picture this past event or person as a chain that is connected to an anchor. Feel the weight of it pulling you down, anchoring you.

Step 3: Now, imagine letting go of that chain. Picture yourself cutting it loose, releasing the anchor, or simply letting it drift away. As you do, allow yourself to release this past event or person emotionally.

Let yourself drift up into the sky in your imagination. As you do, you'll feel so much lighter. This isn't some magic. It's a tool that helps you really feel the weight that past events have been weighing heavily on your mental and physical self. And here's the beauty of it: You can use this to let go of any past event or person every single time it pops back up.

Now, sometimes you might need to face the event first before you can properly let it go, especially if there are things you haven't fully healed from yet. But honestly, even the stuff I thought I'd dealt with has come back around on repeat. This tool? It's a game-changer for breaking the cycle and letting that sh*t go for good.

And remember, *consistency is key*. Just because you've done this practice once doesn't mean your problems will magically disappear overnight. It's a conscious, ongoing cycle of letting go and healing. Keep showing up for yourself. Keep doing the work. That's where the real change happens.

'The past is dead and no longer exists, so don't allow your past to steal your present and future.'

WHEN TO SURRENDER

'Surrendering isn't always negative; it means being okay with not controlling one's life and path'

Surrendering to your subconscious is one of the most freeing and liberating things you can do.
Surrendering isn't always bad; sometimes, surrendering simply means letting go of trying to control things we can't control.

Instead of stressing or overthinking, let thoughts come to you instead of trying to find them. Like Alan Watts, an English writer from the 1915s, said,

"When we talk constantly, we never hear what anyone else has to say. And so, in exactly the same way, if we think all the time, we don't have anything to think about except thoughts." He said that in his lecture 'The Art of Meditation' in the early 1960s.'

When we surrender, we allow our higher self to make the decisions, which is our intuition at work. It can be so easy to control every aspect of our lives and future; our minds are so busy thinking, planning, and analysing that we forget to let go and allow more natural wisdom to come through our higher selves.

If you understand or have read about mindfulness, this is all about letting your mind be still and silent to allow thoughts and ideas to come to you. This can be tricky if you like to control situations. Even though it doesn't seem like it, you are in complete control by letting go and feeling. Sometimes, *we believe the answer is within somebody else, but it's within you.* Nobody else knows your situation, thoughts or feelings better than you.

But we all need a bit of help from time to time.

Did you know our subconscious mind cannot create new information? This is why and how we get stuck in blind spots. We get caught up in our own perspectives and cannot see it any other way until we learn new information.

We all could use a little help and guidance. Let's call it inspiration! The best place to find these seeds is in books. It is great to read/listen to many other people on the same frequency level as you (people who resonate with you). Then, take bits and pieces from them and create your own beliefs, habits, and coping mechanisms. This is how I have created happiness, peace, love, freedom, success, and many other great human feelings. It's important to remember we are all different people, and when reading books and getting knowledge from others, you should create your own beliefs within them instead of taking on others' beliefs as your own.

We cannot know everything; it's simply impossible. Saying 'I don't know' is a hell of a lot more powerful than I know.

 Embracing the idea that we can't and won't know everything creates space to learn. It's amazing that people are out there helping, guiding, making a huge impact, and even achieving financial freedom simply by sharing the knowledge they already have. There's a kind of magic in that. To do the same, we must be willing to let go of the need to control every detail. Just believe in yourself, trust that you're enough, and be open to the guidance and ideas that come your way.

Let go. Drop it. Be free. When we release that need to know it all, we open ourselves up to breakthroughs and the actions that lead us to fulfilment and freedom.

Surrendering to not knowing exactly how your life will turn out, having an idea of where you want to go but obsessing over it and not allowing the flow of life to take its course may leave you feeling stressed.

Surrendering to the realisation that you cannot control others' thoughts, emotions, or actions is a powerful step towards personal growth.

Often, we become entangled in frustration or disappointment when others don't behave as we expect or desire. This can happen in many contexts, such as when a family member isn't contributing around the house or someone isn't saying what we want to hear. The key is to allow others to be themselves and to shift your focus back to your own life, goals, and commitments. Instead of being heavily invested in their lives, choose to stay in your own lane. Doing so can foster a more harmonious environment and cultivate a sense of inner calm.

'Expect nothing and appreciate everything'

But what happens when the frustration isn't with others? It's with life itself?

Have you ever started something like a project, a relationship, or even a new chapter in your life, and it felt like everything was working against you? Like, no matter how much effort you put in, things kept going wrong? I'm not talking about the usual ups and downs that come with life. I mean those moments when *every little thing* feels unnecessarily difficult, where simple tasks somehow spiral into chaos, and it feels like the universe is throwing roadblock after roadblock at you.

When we hold on too tightly to an idea or outcome, pride or ego can trick us into clinging to something that ultimately becomes a burden. That's exactly what happened to me. I held onto a business I'd been building for years, even though *everything* was going wrong toward the end. I was so focused on controlling my life and business that I created nothing but resistance. From my experience, if you ignore your intuition, whether you call it your higher self, the universe, God, or Mother Nature, something will step in and force you to face the truth you've been avoiding.

This is the true art of letting go and surrendering; if it's not working, it doesn't feel right, and it is causing stress and outer and inner conflict, then maybe deep down, you know this is not the path for you. Holding your hands up and walking away from something that isn't aligned with you is powerful! Some people find themselves stuck in situations where they feel obligated to stay and do certain things, even when it's not truly right for them. The idea of simply walking away can seem daunting or wrong.

However, I assure you that something or someone genuinely aligned with your purpose will come to you in divine timing. Trusting in divine timing is essential because once you understand that you are always exactly where you need to be, it becomes easier to let go and move on. You will realise that divine timing is always working in your favour.

Grab your notepad and pen and start free-writing about letting go and surrendering; write and allow it to flow using this question.

What can I start to let go and surrender to?

Maybe it's a relationship, a friendship, a family member, a job, a house, or maybe you are ready to surrender to others' actions and the words they speak. You could let go of a person or an unpleasant event that happened to you in the past.

Maybe you get angry or stressed when someone doesn't act in a manner you prefer. Let go and surrender to the fact that it's not your life, not your journey!

The energy you will save by doing this will help you stay focused on your own path.

'Surrendering to the realisation that you cannot control others' thoughts, emotions, or actions is a powerful step towards personal peace and growth.'

MAGIC MORNING ROUTINE

'Morning routines set the tone for the day and prime you for success.'

Morning routines saved my energetic life. They have helped me cultivate motivation and channel my energy into feelings of empowerment and self-belief. Thanks to these routines, I've learned to appreciate what I have while also manifesting the things and feelings I truly want.

I would wake up just five minutes before I 'had to' leave, running around in a panic to get ready, eat, and dash out the door. Now, waking up 1- 2 hours earlier and starting my day with meditation, stretching, walking, reading, and journaling. No more rushing or stressing. My mornings are calm and intentional. This routine keeps me aligned with the success and opportunities I'm after, and it's incredible how this shift has transformed my life. It's all about setting the right tone for the day ahead!

If you want to feel some clarity, go on with your day with a clear mind and great energy, be calm and see the beauty in everything and anything, then I suggest starting your day with a magic morning.

A magic morning routine is a powerful way to elevate your energy and start each day with purpose. It keeps you motivated, fuels your momentum, and aligns your body, mind, and spirit to help you feel balanced and ready to take on anything that comes your way. By crafting a routine that works for you, you create positive energy and set a clear direction for your day. Instead of draining yourself by thinking about what needs to get done, you save that energy and channel it toward growth, clarity, and success. With a magic morning, you're not just preparing for the day but empowering yourself to thrive in it.

I never had a structure in my life when I was at my lowest. Without some structure or routine in the morning, you feel slow and take a while to get into the day. Mornings are to feed your soul; let me say that again...

'Mornings are to FEED your soul.'

You can feed your soul in many ways, such as through meditation, reading, walking, exercising, or writing down gratitude and affirmations, which I will include at the end of this chapter. As we touched on in these last chapters, setting clear intentions is everything when it comes to using these tools. It's not about half-heartedly going through the motions and expecting magic to just show up. It's about 'feeling' it, knowing exactly 'why' you're doing these magic mornings and putting that purpose into every action. When we set strong intentions, we amplify the impact, making it all that much more powerful. Establishing a morning routine has been a transformative experience for me. It gives me a sense of purpose and gives me time for myself; now, this is an excellent way to start the day!

The reason to begin your day using tools like these is to cultivate a positive mindset. This is particularly beneficial if you are currently struggling with your thoughts and emotions.

Not everyone's morning routine will look the same, and as you grow and evolve, so will your routine. In this chapter, you'll create a morning ritual that energises and empowers you. Your "magic morning" will transform with you over time, keeping things fresh and exciting. It's okay to add new elements that inspire you. Just make sure you plan ahead the night before to keep the flow. The most important thing is consistency. Even if you don't feel like it, commit to doing your routine. Notice how it uplifts your mood and mindset throughout the day. And if you miss a day, don't dwell on it. Instead, pay attention to how it affects your day and use that awareness to grow.

Each morning is a new opportunity to align yourself with your highest potential!

Morning routines that set the tone for my day:

- Wake up, grab a book, and dive into a few pages of inspiration. Then, journal what I'm grateful for; it's a game-changer for my mindset.
- Wake up, head into the woods for a walk, flow through some yoga, listen to a guided meditation,

and then journal. I often ask myself a thought-provoking question and let the words flow. Oh, and my high-vibe playlist? A non-negotiable, it instantly lifts my mood.

- Wake up, meditate, stretch it out, and write down my affirmations. If something's weighing on my mind, I'll journal it out, process the emotions, and release the stress.
- Wake up, breathe in nature on a woodland walk, come back to yoga, journal, and end by soaking up the wisdom of a great book.

I always start my mornings with some kind of movement, learning, or self-connection, whether it's journaling or meditation. This is because life, our minds, social media, and other people's energies and opinions can feel suffocating. When I start my day grounded in what I want to achieve, in my intentions, and in my true purpose to help and inspire others, I know I won't lose my way.

We also hold so much stress in our bodies, especially on our shoulders and necks. When stress hormones flood our system, one of the first reactions is tense muscles. Holistic therapy teaches that releasing that physical tension through movement also frees up stuck energy, creating a ripple effect on our mental and emotional well-being.

For me, learning is key. I'm a big believer in the idea that 'knowledge is power.' We can learn so much from others who've walked the path we're on or achieved things we're working toward. Sure, you can figure it out on your own, but why not get inspired and gain insights from those who've already found their way? It's all about setting ourselves up for success.

One of the most transformative habits I've embraced is waking up earlier. Yes, I know waking up early might sound terrifying, like the stuff of nightmares for some. But trust me, it's worth it!

Like I said, there is no wrong or right, and you don't have to do anything, including waking up early. However, waking up earlier than I used to has changed the dynamic of my whole day and life. Most mornings, I wake up before people get up in my house, which means I have a good hour or two to be alone with myself and get into a productive, calm, positive, and energetic mindset. What is early or earlier? An hour earlier than you usually do. This allows you to go through your magic morning without rushing.

When I was at my lowest point mentally, I NEVER woke up early. I used to be so bad that when I was at university, I had a part-time job in a coffee shop, meaning that I would have to arrive at 5:30 am to open the shop at 6 am. I'd get my mum to phone me repeatedly from 5 am until I woke up. If I could, I would have easily slept in until noon, and sometimes I did. I would wake up feeling groggy, unmotivated, sad and confused, and oversleeping left me feeling like crap; then, if that weren't enough, I would spend 10-30 minutes scrolling on social media first thing in the morning!

Some days, I genuinely don't want to get out of bed, no deep reason, no dramatic backstory, just because my bed is heaven, plain and simple! And let's be honest, you probably feel the same. Who doesn't love staying wrapped up in that cosy, safe little cocoon?

But here's what I know: the benefits of getting up and starting my magic morning completely outweigh the short-lived comfort of staying wrapped up.

When we're building a better, more productive life, sometimes we have to lean into what brings us real, long-term happiness rather than just short-term ease. So, yeah, the short-term comfort might be staying in bed and skipping my morning routine. But the long-term pays off! Waking up early to fuel my mindset, charge my energy, and set myself up for a successful day. It's the difference between a small moment of comfort and building the kind of life where you meet your financial goals, hit your stride, and feel that true, lasting fulfilment and alignment. PHONES BEFORE BED AND FIRST THING IN THE MORNING...

I can not express enough that scrolling through social media or even going on your phone last thing at night or first thing in the morning is poison for your brain, especially when you are struggling mentally.

Why? The last thing we should be looking at or focusing on is other people's lives. Remember, our mornings are for ourselves to *feed our souls.* We are so susceptible to information first thing in the morning and last thing at night that filling these moments with pure personal development will benefit us more than subconsciously comparing our lives to others. Not only that, but what you see on social media is out of your control, which means starting your morning with an upsetting, demotivating, or annoying post can set you up for a pretty rubbish day.

Take the power back in your life and set some boundaries for social media time.

NOTE PAD TIME! Grab your notepad and pen, and let's design your new morning routine together!

Bringing the Mind, Body, and Spirit into your morning routine is key to creating balance and flow in your life. Keep it simple, choose one thing from each aspect that feels right for *you*, and start your day with intention:

Mind

- **Journaling** – Brain dump, gratitude or intention-setting, gratitude, affirmations
- **Reading** – A few pages of a book that expands your mindset
- **Affirmations** – Speaking powerful, positive beliefs into existence

Body

- **Stretching/Yoga** – Loosening up tension and increasing energy
- **Cold Shower** – Wakes you up and boosts mental resilience
- **Movement** – Walk in nature, work-out, or dance to high-vibe music

Spirit

- **Meditation** – Even 5-10 minutes to connect with yourself
- **Breathwork** – Calms the nervous system and resets your energy

- **Visualisation** – Seeing yourself already living your dream life

Next, set a wake-up time that feels right. Maybe it's 6 a.m., perhaps it's 6:30 a.m. Whatever fits your rhythm. And if these ideas don't quite resonate, feel free to create your own mini-routine! Like I said before, an hour before, you would normally get up.

Now, write it down in your journal, planner, or calendar as a commitment to yourself:

"I, [your name], make a declaration that I will wake up at [chosen time] every morning and complete my magic morning."

Then, jot down your routine so it's ready to go.

There is no wrong or right way to plan or do your morning routine. Like I said before, if you miss a day, please don't beat yourself up; observe your day and see how you feel. When I miss a magic morning, I feel deflated and fall back into unhelpful thought patterns. Like I said, there is no wrong or right way. Some people don't like planning things to a T, and others do, but planning a day ahead is a magic trick that will 100% help you. You know what I'm going to say... *FOLLOW THE*

PATH OF LESS RESISTANCE. I have tried following the path I thought I should follow, and it burned me out!

These can be incorporated into your journalling, which we will dive into later.

Examples of affirmations, declarations and gratitude:

Affirmations
- I am so lucky
- Today, I will listen to what I need
- Today, I will listen to my body
- Everything I want is on its way to me
- I am beautiful

Declarations
- I promise I will listen to myself
- I promise to be kind to myself
- I will love myself like I love my family or friends

Gratitude
- I am grateful for my meeting going well today
- I am grateful for my heart that works for me every day
- I am grateful to my partner, who always supports me
- I am grateful that I woke up in the morning
- I am grateful for a safe journey to work today
- I am grateful for that sale I will make today

Affirmation meaning - An affirmation is a positive statement you repeat to yourself to promote a positive mindset and belief system. It can help improve your self-esteem, reduce stress and anxiety, increase motivation and productivity, and help you achieve personal goals.

Declaration means the act of making an official statement about something: the act of declaring

Gratitude means a feeling of appreciation and thankfulness towards someone or something. It involves acknowledging the goodness in our lives and recognising that it comes from outside of ourselves.

You may find one that works better for you. When I purely used affirmations, sometimes it would make me feel like I was lying to myself, so I used declarations, meaning I made a promise to myself instead of 'pretending to do or have something'. But like I said and will continue to say, we are all different with unique minds. That's why you choose what works best for you and your personality. Play around with it, chop and change and remember to enjoy the process and become aware of how you feel after doing a week of magic mornings!

When creating affirmations for yourself, using words that resonate with you and fit naturally into your everyday language is crucial. This makes the affirmations more effective, as your subconscious mind will recognise and accept them, making them easier to get into the subconscious mind.

For example, you might hear an affirmation like, "I am the divine god/goddess that magnetises everything good to me." While it sounds mystical and positive, it might not be effective if you don't typically use such language. Instead, pay attention to the words you commonly use. If your affirmation is about money, consider what limiting statements you frequently say, such as "I don't have money," and transform them into positive affirmations like "I have money." "I'm not good enough." To "I am good enough and deserve love."

Using affirmations that align with your usual vocabulary makes them more impactful. For instance, "Money is divine and is always mine" is a powerful affirmation, but if those words feel unnatural to you, they might not work as effectively. Instead, choose affirmations that feel authentic and relatable to you. Adding specific actions to your affirmations can also enhance their effectiveness. This helps you see tangible progress and reinforces the new beliefs you are trying to cultivate. For example:

"I love myself and everyone around me. My action is to look in the mirror and tell myself how beautiful I am. I will also show my appreciation and love to others by being

open and honest about how grateful I am to have them in my life."

This approach makes it clear to your mind that you are responsible for creating these new pathways in your life. If all that overwhelms or confuses you, simply wake up an hour earlier than usual and write three things you are grateful for every morning. See how you get on for a week and then return to this chapter. I know change can sometimes be overwhelming, but change helps us grow. I believe in you! You've got this.

'Using affirmations that align with your usual vocabulary makes them more impactful.'

WHAT IS SUCCESS

'Success isn't one-size-fits-all; it's about defining your own path and thriving on your terms.'

I spent years of my life chasing 'success', only to realise that what I'd been chasing for years wasn't even my version of success. I was living someone else's dream, building businesses in the beauty and aesthetics industry, and making fantastic money, but at what cost? I was out of the house from morning till night, stuck in one room treating clients day after day. It didn't matter how much I made in a week, a day, or even an hour; deep down, I knew this life wasn't truly a 'successful' life to me.

The moment I stopped looking for success in someone else's version and started defining it on my own terms, life reached a whole new level, and I felt a sense of purpose and alignment I'd never experienced before.

Success is a perception; just like 'good enough' and 'perfect', these words have many meanings to each and every individual. When we see success, it can be easy to get consumed by other people's perspectives of success. If this happens, it's easy to find yourself unconsciously mimicking and reflecting on others' methods, businesses, and lives. But if success has a unique and different meaning, like every human on this planet, then there is not one road to success.

To me, success was no longer working from 7 am to 9 pm, dealing with clients who didn't appreciate my time.

We evolve and adapt; we are meant to change. I would work out how many hours it took per client to make more than what I was making the previous month.

At the beginning of my business, I was amazed at how much I could make, but then I slowly realised I would have to work 7 am-9 pm six days a week every week to make the maximum money I could make. Not to mention all the business bills and rent that came along with it all and the work itself having a massive impact on my body. I began to scale the businesses, but something didn't feel right, and things started to go wrong. If it wasn't my manufacturer sending the wrong items, it was my employee not showing up. It felt like a domino effect, with one thing after another going wrong.

As I mentioned earlier, when we ignore what feels right, the universe has a way of making things harder and will eventually step in to set things straight, one way or another. I finally admitted… I was unhappy and living someone else's dream and life.

It came to my attention that I was trading my precious time on earth for money by carrying out beauty treatments. What once seemed like a success started to feel like a waste, a sellout to my true divine purpose of helping others. Don't get me wrong, there's nothing wrong with being in any industry if you truly love what you do, but I realised it wasn't aligned with me anymore. I never intended to enter the beauty world; it found me through my brother's ex-fiancée, and I was drawn by the money I could make. But I hadn't considered what I'd be doing day in and day out. It was purely about the money, and now I've learned to value something much deeper:

Sell from your soul, not selling your soul.

This was not what success meant to me, especially doing something I wasn't passionate about. I no longer vibrated on the same frequency as this lifestyle, and I didn't want to have to be somewhere at a particular time to make my money.

The true vibration I was on was remote working, which means working from anywhere in the world, and passive income, which means making one thing like an online course, a book or a digital download that sells repeatedly.

Remember, *you are not obligated to be the same person you were last week, this week, or yesterday.*
This is where I became stuck for years; I thought I was obligated to carry on in the businesses that were making me miserable because of the money, effort and time I had built for years, *but we are forever evolving.*

I felt ashamed and guilty like I'd let my family down. They believed in me, supported me, and even helped fund my business when I started. They were so proud, telling everyone how well I was doing. So, when my Auntie passed, and I decided to shut everything down, enough was enough.

I got my parents together, a rare event in itself, and told them I was unhappy. I apologised, explained that I was closing the business I'd worked so hard to build, and finally told them about the life coaching and mental health course I'd been secretly taking. I braced myself for disappointment, a lecture, or those looks that say, *You've failed us*. But instead, they told me they understood. They said they were proud of me regardless and that it was normal to outgrow things.
I cried. I cried out of relief and out of sadness. Relief because they didn't see me as a failure. Sadness because I never got the chance to tell my Auntie about this new venture before she suddenly passed.

It was a gut-punch reminder that tomorrow isn't promised. So, if something matters to you, don't hold back. Say it, do it, live it, because regret isn't something you can take back.

WHAT DOES SUCCESS MEAN TO YOU?

So, what does success mean to you? I encourage you to explore this question not just once but multiple times over your lifetime. That one question changed my life in 48 hours, and it helped me realise that we all have different answers and that there is no wrong or right way to be successful.

The first coach I had was an online beauty business coach; when she asked us these questions in a training video, my life was never the same. Not only did I slowly start to detach myself from the multiple businesses I had grown, but I also detached myself from the meaning I had given 'success'.

This is off-topic, but we live in a remarkable world where we can be and do whatever we want; we all have our social media platforms. Again, this is about CHOICE and how we use these platforms. Do you choose to watch brain cell-killing videos that bring nothing to your life and scroll for hours, achieving nothing? OR do you choose to follow people with knowledge and wisdom to help you grow and feed your brain what it needs and deserves?

Before social media, you would have to be with some modelling agency to get modelling jobs; now, you can pay for headshots and create a social modelling platform. Thanks to social media, you no longer need to be spotted singing in bars; you can make a social media platform to become spotted. This could be applied to most things in this day and age; all it takes is one post to go viral.

You can do anything you want and know how you start...? You just start. If you want to have a social food blog, think of a catchy name and just do it! Even if you're not 100% with the name, you can always change it (this is called CCIIA, something we will get into in a later chapter). The important thing is just to start. I never thought it was essential to create something that you are truly passionate about, but learning about the power of vibration is the key to true abundance and success.

I tell you this because we have more opportunities now than ever before, and it's up to us to use social media to our advantage.

What does success mean to you?

Get your journal out and start to play around with the meaning you hold to this word.

- Is success to you, spending time with family, finishing all the housework and cooking? Because that's great!

- Is success to you, earning X amount of money and working less?

- Is success to you getting your dream job?

- Is success to you simply holding your energy high and helping others?

There is no wrong or right, better or worse, good or bad; your meaning of these words is good enough! The whole point of life is to feel emotions, learn new things and create a successful life, whatever that may look or feel like to you. Don't allow social media to warp your version of success because the person you are watching on the screen is not you; they will have different morals and have lived a different life, so what they find 'successful' may not be what you find to be successful.

I can't express this enough: we are all different, and that is why I do not believe in right or wrong, not only in success but in life itself. Each of us has our own unique perspectives on life, words, and situations. By being authentic and true to yourself, you will create your own kind of success. This authenticity frees you from constantly looking to others for how to become successful.

Even though one might say, "This is the way to make X amount of money," remember that this is just one of countless paths. There are a million ways to achieve whatever you want, and your path will always suit you better than following someone else's path.

I want to touch on something I keep bringing up: the idea that there's no such thing as right and wrong. Now, don't get me wrong; this doesn't mean I believe anyone can just do whatever they want without regard for others or causing harm. That's not what I'm saying.
Think about it… Most arguments happen because two or more people disagree on what's "right" or "wrong." These concepts are often rooted in perspective, not universal truth. For example, I personally don't believe in eating meat or animal products, but someone else might feel it's completely right for them because of their own values or reasoning. Another example could be religion. What feels sacred and "right" to one person might feel entirely different for someone with a different faith.

That's why I prefer to frame things as *moral* or *immoral* or as *empowering* versus *disempowering*. It shifts the focus from a rigid black-and-white view to one that's more layered and personal to each of us. It's about finding alignment with your own values, not imposing them on others.

'Don't allow social media to warp your version of success.'

CELEBRATING YOUR WINS

'Where your focus goes, your energy flows.'
- Tony Robbins

I once heard someone say, "It doesn't matter how successful you are. You could be the richest person in the world, in every sense of the word, but if you don't celebrate your wins, you will always feel like a loser."

That hit me hard because it's true. Success without acknowledgement is empty. It's like climbing a mountain only to stare at the next peak without appreciating how far you've come.

It's so easy to get caught up in the "what's next?" mindset.

Housework needs doing, deadlines are looming, and there's always something else waiting for your attention. You tick things off the list and move straight on, barely noticing the progress you've made. But here's the thing:

when all your energy is focused on what you still need to do, and you never stop acknowledging what you've achieved, it's easy to lose sight of your success. You end up chasing more and more, but it's never enough. The truth is that your brain thrives on what you feed it. If all it hears is, "There's still so much to do," it will amplify the pressure and stress.

But if you take a moment to recognise and celebrate your wins, you'll feel more motivated, energised, and ready for what's next.

Celebrating your wins, no matter how small, triggers your brain to release dopamine, that feel-good chemical. This isn't just about feeling good in the moment. It reinforces positive behaviour and creates a feedback loop: the more you celebrate, the more motivated you feel to keep going. When you skip celebrating, your brain doesn't register your efforts as valuable. Over time, this can lead to burnout, lack of motivation, and even resentment toward your goals. Celebrating isn't just a "nice thing to do"; it's essential for long-term success.

We often wait for the 'big' wins to celebrate, like landing a dream client, hitting a major milestone, or launching a new project. But what about the smaller victories? Sending that email you've been putting off, sticking to your daily routine, or even taking a break when needed.

These moments matter, too. Success is built on small, intentional steps, and each deserves recognition.

One of the biggest traps we fall into is comparing our wins to others'. You might think, "Why should I celebrate this when someone else just achieved something so much bigger?" But their journey isn't yours. Your wins are meaningful because they represent progress in your story. When you stop comparing, you start valuing what you've achieved. This shift isn't just freeing; it's empowering. Your path is unique, and every step forward is worth celebrating, not because of how it measures up but because it matters to you.

Celebrating your wins doesn't have to mean throwing a party or spending money. It's about taking a moment to acknowledge your effort and progress. It can be as simple as reflecting in a journal, writing down what you accomplished and how it made you feel, telling a friend, family member, or mentor about your win, or even treating yourself to your favourite meal, a relaxing break, or something small that feels rewarding.

It's important to celebrate your wins daily. I tend to do this in the evening, and doing so will get you into the habit and routine, making this second nature while reaping all the benefits.

Success is worth celebrating, as life's too short to let your wins slip by unnoticed. I know I did, and I lost years of my life in the process. Celebrating isn't just about enjoying the moment; it's about cultivating a mindset of gratitude and growth. When you celebrate your progress, you create momentum, stay motivated, and feel more fulfilled. So, the next time you achieve something big or small, pause. Take a deep breath. Smile. You've earned it.

'Success isn't just about the destination; it's about appreciating every step of the journey.'

MONEY: A MAN-MADE ENERGY

'Money is neither good nor bad; it's what you do with it that makes the difference.'

Let's talk about money. For years, I believed 'money is the root of all evil' because that's what I was taught growing up. But here's the thing: if you believe something is evil, why would you want it in your life? That belief alone can block us from attracting it in the first place. Money isn't evil; it's energy, and like any energy, it flows where we focus our attention.

When I first heard the idea that money is energy, I thought it was ridiculous. It's not alive, so how could it possibly be energy? But then I learned that it's *us*, our thoughts, feelings, words, and actions, that give money its energetic charge. Your relationship with money reflects your perspective. The thought loop I've shared before applies here: what you think affects how you feel, which affects what you say and do. If you believe money is hard to earn, guess what? It will be. But if you shift that belief by telling yourself, "I love making money", and be open-minded about money, you'll see new opportunities come your way.

Here's a practical example: I don't like using the word 'expensive. ' What's 'expensive,' anyway? It's all about perspective. Something pricey to one person might be pocket-changed to another. When we call something 'too expensive,' we might be signalling to our minds that it's out of reach. Instead, I say, "I'm choosing to spend my money differently right now." It's subtle but shifts your mindset from lack to choice.

Money and happiness. Now, let's address the big one: *'Money doesn't buy happiness.'* I used to roll my eyes at this. Coming from a family with financial struggles, I thought money *had* to be the answer to happiness. But after receiving an unexpected inheritance, I learned the hard way that it's not. Money can ease stress and provide security, but it doesn't heal emotional wounds or fix relationships. Those things require inner work.

When I stopped obsessing over money and chasing it relentlessly, something incredible happened: opportunities to earn began flowing to me naturally. By letting go of the pressure and focusing on what truly fulfilled me, the path became so much clearer.

Money Isn't the Villain

Here's the truth: money is neutral. It doesn't make people good or bad; it simply amplifies who they already are. Kind people will do good things with money, while selfish people... well, you get the idea. Wanting wealth doesn't make you greedy or immoral. It's okay to want financial freedom, even if others try to guilt you for it.

I'll leave you with this: Don't let other people's beliefs about money hold you back. Whether it's family, friends, or societal conditioning, their opinions aren't your truth. Work on your inner happiness first because when you feel good inside, everything flows more easily on the outside.

The bottom line?

- Money won't make you happy, but it can make life easier.

- Wanting wealth doesn't make you a bad person.

- Focus on inner growth first, and the rest will follow in divine timing.

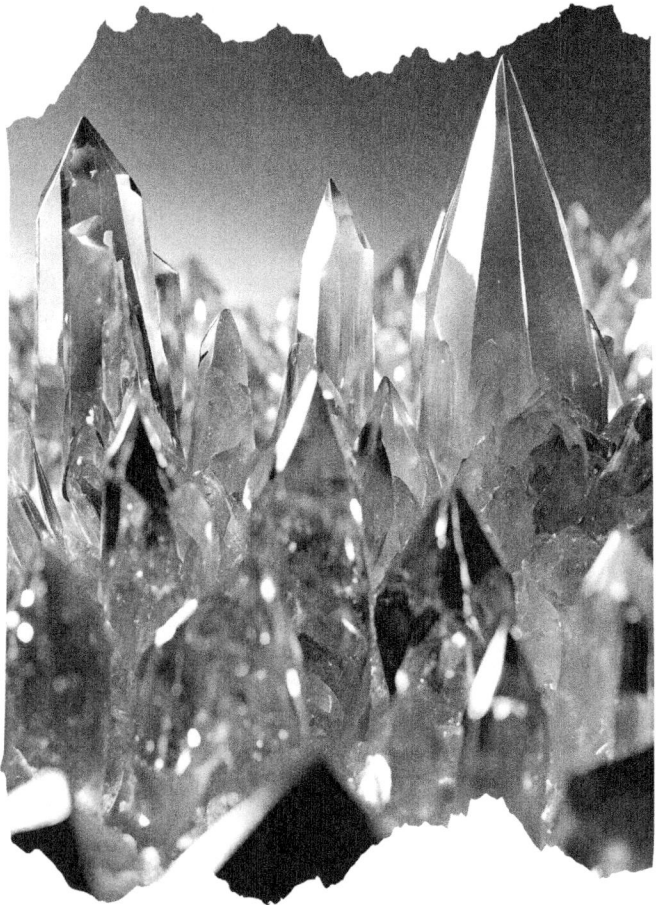

BECOMING YOUR OWN BEST FRIEND

∞

'Becoming your own best friend is a journey worth taking, communication is the key, especially with ourselves.'

I used to be my own worst enemy, constantly bullying myself and tearing myself down. I was never my own cheerleader, just the voice in my head that always found fault. No matter what I accomplished, I'd focus on what I hadn't done, never celebrating the small wins. I'd convince myself that I was annoying, that no one really liked me or cared about what I had to say. This went on for years.

It wasn't until I started learning that the things we hear and say warp our reality that everything changed. I began journaling, not just writing down my feelings but having real conversations with myself, pen to paper. Just like communication is key to any relationship, this stands for the relationship with ourselves, too. By changing that inner dialogue, I started building a healthier, more supportive relationship with myself, and it's been life-changing.

The thing is, we're born alone and die alone; you are the only one in your head, and no one else will understand you or know you as much as you do. We get lost in life for many reasons, but one of the biggest killers of our identity is **not being authentic to ourselves.**

It's important to talk to yourself to create and build a relationship. I was raised in a generation that thought talking to yourself was the first sign of madness, but I promise you that's a lie!

'Becoming your own best friend is the best thing you will ever do.'

If you don't know how to start building a relationship with yourself, maybe you find it uncomfortable to talk out loud, or you get confused working things out in your head, then at first, I would highly recommend journaling.

What is journaling, how do you do it, and why is it important? Ask yourself questions, write out your feelings and events that have happened, and preferably write them down regularly. It is expected not to be 100% with yourself at first. Our ego likes to take over, but after time and consistency, it will get easier. This way, you will know what you desire the most by listening to yourself and communicating. You will start to see your thought patterns, know what kind of moods you are in, and even the reason why.

I recently had the pleasure of collaborating with Dr. Millan, a former GP of 15 years who transitioned into stress management coaching. We had an in-depth conversation about journaling, which he humorously referred to as 'brain dumping' (yes, I laughed; I couldn't help it). He explained that one of the biggest benefits of

daily journaling is creating more mental space. When we free up space in our minds, we can problem-solve more effectively, reducing cognitive pressure and stress.
Every single one of my clients has told me how simply putting pen to paper has been life-changing in so many ways. It's such a straightforward habit, yet the impact it can have is profound.

We've all heard the saying, *'Communication is the key.'* This isn't just for relationships; communicating with yourself will help you reach mental clarity and a better, well-rounded mindset.

We can get lost when we stop listening, connecting, and communicating with ourselves. The easiest way to connect with ourselves is through questions.

Here are a few questions you can journal on:

- What does my perfect day look like?

- If nothing else mattered, what would I want to do with my life?

- If I could do any job, what would it be?

- What do I enjoy doing in my spare time?

- What could I do today to feel more alive?

- Have I had a good day? If so, what made it good? If not, what can I do differently next time?

- What can I do to have more fun and bring more joy into my life?

- What emotions or thoughts am I holding onto that no longer serve me?

- How am I feeling today?

- What could make me feel better right now?

- Looking back at that argument earlier, what happened, and what have I learned from it?

- What have I achieved today, this week, or this month?

- What are my core values, and how can I live more aligned with them?

These questions are meant to encourage self-awareness, emotional clarity, and personal growth. Reflecting on them regularly can help you stay connected to your true self and purpose.

You can ask yourself as many questions as you like, as only you know what questions need an answer. When you have answered yourself, look at your life and compare it with your answers. If your life is far from how you desire it to be, make some changes by writing down what you can do more or less to achieve your desired life. Doing the same things day in and day out will get us the same outcomes; we need to make changes, even if they are small, to live a happier, better life.

I do this exercise because it's important to know what you want from life. You are your best friend, after all. It's important to grow that deeper connection with yourself. Not only by meditating and exercising but knowing who you are and what the f*ck you want from your life… why? Because you deserve it. Think about someone you love and consider your best friend. Wouldn't you want them to have their ideal life?

If you don't know what you want, how are you meant to get it?

Some people may understand and pick up the meaning and point behind journaling, but when I was taught this tool, no one explained the reasoning behind WHY and for me, that makes all the difference to understanding why I am doing something and what the benefits are.

Journalling is simply having a conversation with yourself, a check-up. One day, it may be sweet and short; another day, you may be 2-4 pages in.

I like to journal every morning, and sometimes, there are no points to my journaling. I'm not doing it with intentions or to search for anything; I'm simply communicating with myself and making a conviction. Some days, I start with, 'Hey Pix, How are you feeling?' Then words flow, and I end up feeling inspired!

I used to avoid journaling because I thought there was a 'right' or 'wrong' way to do it. I thought there was some secret formula I needed to follow. But honestly, all you really need to do is pick up a pen, start writing, and watch your relationship with yourself unfold. It's not about perfection; it's about getting real, letting your thoughts flow, and giving yourself the space to reflect and grow.

Treat yourself with respect by speaking kindly and nurturing yourself because all we genuinely want is for someone to tell us we are doing a great job, and what better person to give that support than ourselves?

Now that we've covered building a strong relationship with yourself let's talk about how to maintain that level of inner peace and self-love without allowing external forces to disrupt it. If you don't take charge of your internal barriers, the world around you can easily break you down or insult you. This means that sh*tty people's energies, words and events can affect us in a disempowering way. That's why creating and enforcing boundaries, both with others and with yourself, is crucial. It's not just about protecting yourself from others' negativity but about setting the standard for how you treat yourself.

'If you don't respect your own boundaries, no one else will.'

For example, if you have a boundary that says, 'I don't allow anyone, including myself, to speak to me in a disrespectful way,' it's vital that you uphold this rule. You must treat yourself with the same kindness and respect you would expect from a close friend. When you consistently honour your boundaries, it becomes much easier to enforce them with others.

Once you've built a strong bond with yourself where you truly love, accept, and respect who you are, why let someone else's judgments or unhappiness affect your peace? You've cultivated this inner strength, this friendship with yourself, so don't let anyone, whether it be family, friends, or strangers, diminish that. Your opinion of yourself is the only one that truly matters.

People often project their negativity onto others because they're unhappy with themselves. Don't let their misery influence your happiness or self-worth. You've earned this power; now, protect it. Let me offer another perspective here: we can't change other people. We can't control what they say or how they act. But as my mother always told me, *"You can't change how people behave; you can only change how you respond."*

For example, let's say you have someone in your life who disrespects you or speaks to you unkindly. You've stood up for yourself countless times and tried every way you can think of to address the situation. But despite their behaviour, you love them, and cutting them out of your life isn't an option for you.

In situations like this, it's crucial to do two things:

1. **Don't let their energy affect you.** Recognise that their hurtful behaviour says more about *them* than it does about you. They're operating from a place of their own pain or struggles, not because of who you are.

2. **Shift your reaction.** Instead of letting their words or actions dictate how you feel, focus on maintaining your peace and composure. Respond in a way that aligns with your values, not their negativity.

Not everyone will agree with this approach. I know my partner doesn't. But when you're dealing with difficult, distressed people whom you love and want to keep in your life, it's vital to accept that you can't change them.

The change must come from within you. And when you do that, you'll realise their behaviour has nothing to do with you and everything to do with them.

'Be the friend you've always needed, kind, understanding, and fiercely supportive. When you become your own best friend, you build a foundation of love and strength that helps you thrive, no matter the challenge.'

LYING TO YOURSELF

'You can lie to yourself until your mind believes it, but your soul will always know the truth.'

Here we go! This can be tricky to stop doing, but I promise you that once you do, life will flow.

Let's say you have a friend named Jim, and you invite Jim to your house for dinner. At the last minute, Jim calls and says, "Sorry, I can't come tonight because I've been busy with work." You feel a little hurt because you spent time cooking, but life happens. You ask Jim to come for dinner again, and the same happens! Jim makes another excuse not to come.
Would you have faith in Jim to turn up to dinner again? No, probably not.
Would you trust Jim with your life? Probably not.
Would Jim be your closest friend? Could you rely on Jim when you needed a friend? Nope.

I hope you see where I'm going with this.

When you tell yourself you will do something, then you don't, over and over again, you're not building a trusted relationship with yourself. The relationship you have with yourself will be the same as your relationship with Jim.

This was me through and through. Am I 'perfect'? No, but I am so much better than I was. I used to tell myself I would go to the gym. Did I go? No! Never! If I had listened to myself and built a bond, I would have realised I didn't like going to the gym. I forced myself to think I 'had' to.

Society told me, " All successful people go to the gym." Whatever success means. My partner would tell me to go, so I kept telling myself to go. Was telling myself and forcing myself to go making me like it more? No fricking way! It created war, conflict and resistance deep within.

So you know what I did… I stopped lying to myself and cancelled my membership. For me, being honest with myself mattered more than trying to fit into someone else's idea of success. And the moment I removed that pressure, something magical happened. I started biking and practising yoga, not because I had to, but because I *wanted* to. Then, when the time felt right and I was truly ready, I signed up for the gym again. Now, I go when I *say* I'm going to go. No resistance, just flow.

My point is not to quit exercising altogether; please do not do that. Moving our bodies is extremely good for us in so many ways. I'm pointing out that once you drop the resistance, things you like or resonate with will gravitate towards you.

Drop the "I must" and "I have to" and shift to "I get to".

Let what truly aligns with you come naturally. Look, that's just my story. We often tell ourselves we will do things but never actually follow through. When you align with what feels right for you, the action becomes effortless, and you start to show up in a way that feels genuine. Instead, I started to be consistent with my working out, not because anyone told me to, but because I knew moving my body was not only good for my health but actually to realise built-up stress and energy in my body.

That said, let's say you want to lose weight but don't feel like exercising, or you feel so much resistance towards it that it causes massive internal conflict. Mindset training is key to lifting that resistance. When you train your mind first, everything changes, and your body will naturally follow. It's about aligning your thoughts with your goals so the process becomes less about force and more about flow.

When you tell yourself, "I'll tidy up today," then make an excuse not to, that little voice in your head starts mocking you: "Sure, you say that all the time, but you never follow through."

Each time this happens, you chip away at the trust and connection you have with yourself. Remember, no one expects you to be perfect, and you shouldn't either. What matters is respecting yourself enough to follow through on your intentions. This simple act reduces inner resistance and helps you avoid the frustration and resentment of letting yourself down.

This isn't just about the small stuff; I lied to myself for years about wanting to carry on in my business and created so much conflict with myself by doing something I didn't want to do. Again, the same thing happened: I let go, and my purpose came to me. It was truly beautiful. You can lie to yourself until your mind believes it, but your soul and feelings won't change.

Now, I don't go to the gym, tidy the house or do my magic morning for anyone else but myself. My partner always says, "Move it or lose it", and he is right with that statement!

Where do you go from here?

1. Acknowledge it.
2. Do the things you say you're going to do.
3. If you don't, don't beat yourself up.
4. Feel how not doing it made you feel.
5. Don't say it unless you are 100% going to or not going to.
6. Repeat (until you are consistent with following through).

When you start doing what you say you will, your relationship with yourself will grow, and you will begin to trust yourself.

LOVING YOURSELF

'You yourself, as much as anybody in the entire universe,
deserve your love and affection.'
– Buddha

You may have heard the saying, "You can't love another until you love yourself."
But what does that exactly mean?

Loving yourself means fully accepting yourself. Accept what you have been through, accept what you look and feel like, and then nurture yourself. Speak to yourself with kindness, and respect your own boundaries. Once you fully accept yourself for who you are, you understand that you do not 'need' to change to be the person you want to be.

Once you've made that mindset shift, you can start to look at your actions, habits, and beliefs. But here's the thing: these things aren't you. They are your conditioning; those habits, beliefs, and thought processes have been conditioned. They're layers you've picked up along the way, pieces of you that were conditioned over time. Recognising this helps you see that these patterns don't define you; they're just part of the journey to uncovering who you truly are.

Now, you can see that you are a beautiful human, and your actions, habits, and beliefs are separate. You can allow yourself to shift them while knowing you do not 'need' to change yourself. Instead, you 'get to' change them.

All humans want to feel validated, whether in the things we do, say, or wear in our personal or professional lives. We as humans crave someone saying, "Well done, that was great," or "You look so good today".

Whether you crave feeling sexy, pretty, intelligent, friendly, caring, or loved, I believe there is an aspect of wanting validation to make us feel 'good enough. ' This isn't just about wanting praise; it's about fulfilling a deep need to feel seen, valued, and accepted.

When we look for external validation, whether it's attention, compliments, or recognition, we're setting ourselves up for disappointment. It's not just about getting the feedback we want; external pleasures are usually short-lived and rarely bring long-term fulfilment.

Hear me out for a moment. Imagine you want to feel good about a new hairstyle. You like it, but you also care about others' opinions. Someone compliments your hair, and you feel validated. However, when another person looks at you, you perceive it as a 'bad' stare and start feeling self-conscious, even though you have already received validation from someone else. This feeling of validation is short-term and can easily be affected by others' opinions.

Now, imagine that you couldn't and wouldn't ever care about whatever anyone said about you. Even though, as humans, we all want validation, this time, you give it to yourself. Now, that is a long-term pleasure because no matter what anyone would say, you are happy because you are validating yourself. That can't go away unless you let it by other people's comments and judgments.

I hope you understand where I was going with that. It's okay to want to feel sexy, intelligent, pretty, and caring. As long as you feel it, you will always be it; even if you can't 'feel' it right away, think it until you feel it.

GOOD ENOUGH

'Being good enough doesn't mean being perfect; it means showing up as you are.'

I said it before. Good enough.
People say very often, "I'm not good enough."

To every person who said this to me, I have asked, "What does good enough mean?". Everyone has an entirely different answer. This is because 'good enough' is a perspective, an illusion, a made-up concept from Jenny down the road! You will only be 'good enough' when you choose to be. I've spoken a lot about choices and how our choices create our whole life and that tomorrow isn't promised... so choose in this very moment, for now, and forever, that you are good enough.

You have two choices: let these words pass you by, or go back, soak them in, and commit to taking action. The power to create change starts right here, right now, if you choose it.

YOU ARE GOOD ENOUGH!
SEXY ENOUGH,
KIND ENOUGH,
PRETTY ENOUGH,
LOVABLE ENOUGH,
RICH ENOUGH,
COOL ENOUGH,
FUNKY ENOUGH,
YOU ARE ENOUGH!

Love yourself because relying on the outer world will not give you the long-term pleasure we all want.

I saw this video, and it summed this up pretty well when he said:

'If you look in the mirror and want the reflection to smile, what would you do?'
– Darryl Anka (as Bashar)

SMILE! We are the only ones who can change things in our lives. If you want to be loved and validated... yes, that's right, it all starts with you. The energy you admit will change. People will change around you. Family and friends will notice a difference with you.

Here is an affirmation that may help you:

I am who I am, and that's enough
I AM WHO I AM, AND THAT'S ENOUGH
I AM WHO I AM, AND THAT IS ENOUGH!

EXTERNAL VALIDATION

Many people solely focus on the outer life. As I said before about outside validation, the same goes for people spending a lot of time, money, and energy on external things. I'm not saying having external things is bad, but in my time, I've seen many people spend all their money on the way they look but feel 'broken' inside.

During my years in the beauty industry, it was eye-opening to see how many people would come to me mainly for the 'therapy session,' as they would say. My clients would come to me every other week and spend anywhere from £30-£55. Most clients would spend around £55-£100 per month on their beauty treatments, sometimes more than that. But most of them were so unhappy on the inside. When the conversation on therapy or life coaching came up, many said it was 'too expensive'.

I am in no way judging because I, too, was a little like this. I would buy shoes, clothes, and other external things to make me happy. What did this lead to? Short-term pleasures again.

I started to see a pattern: people were stuck in a loop. A loop of getting beauty treatments to feel good enough or better about themselves, but this wouldn't last long. When they came back, they were in the same emotional state as when they came in the last time. How could they stop the loop of short-term pleasures and bring in long-term pleasures?

I want to tell you one of the best pieces of advice you can and will ever hear. The best thing you can and ever will invest in is yourself. Knowledge truly is 'power. ' By admitting we don't know everything, we will be open to a new perspective in life.

Invest in yourself over a new pair of shoes because outer things may only give you short-term pleasures. I can assure you that investing our time and money into personal development will not only help you but also inspire you, make you happier, more peaceful, and powerful, and give you long-term pleasures; hey, it may even make you more money, so you can buy things you love as well! But it will also help your family, friends and, most importantly, your children if you choose to have them because you will start to shine, and when you walk into that theoretical room, you will brighten even the darkest people around you.

Investing in your self-development could look like buying and reading books like this one. Hiring a life coach, therapist, or mentor, or joining a self-development group/community.

'You do not 'need' to change in order to be the person you want to be.'

OUR THOUGHTS CREATE OUR REALITY

'You are not the storm of your thoughts but the calm observer within.' - Unknown

Hearing this popular statement, 'your thoughts create your reality,' doesn't make it easier for us to change our thoughts and reality. These quotes are amazing, and I will forever live by them, but teaching the logic and the knowledge behind it all will help you to create long-term positive changes in any person's life if they wish to listen.

As humans, we are conditioned. However, we are powerful and can achieve anything we want if we listen and follow our soul/higher self/intuition. Everything will flow when we listen to what's truly right for us.

Now, we all wish a super powerful being would come down and give us all we wish for, but as I explained in the manifesting chapter, it doesn't really work like that.

Our thoughts create our reality; why? Because of the perception we have about the world, which again comes from our conditioning. The more empowering thoughts you have, the more empowered you feel. The more empowered you feel and the more empowering words you say, the more empowering actions you will take.

The same pattern applies to disempowering thoughts; I call this the *Thought Process Loop.*

If you are miserable and negative and have disempowering thoughts, they create disempowering feelings and turn into disempowering actions and behaviours.

Not understanding and learning this loop will hinder your ability to break away from negative outcomes, especially if you were conditioned in a negative household and haven't gotten yourself out of this negative loop.
Here is a simple diagram to help you understand the thought process.

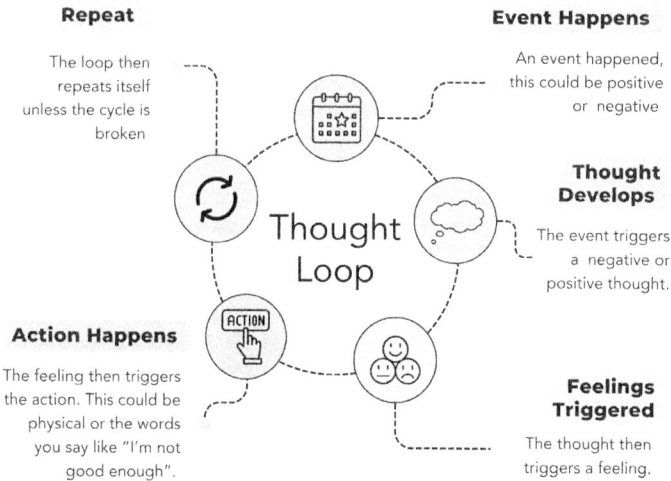

Repeat

The loop then repeats itself unless the cycle is broken

Event Happens

An event happened, this could be positive or negative

Thought Loop

Thought Develops

The event triggers a negative or positive thought.

Action Happens

The feeling then triggers the action. This could be physical or the words you say like "I'm not good enough".

Feelings Triggered

The thought then triggers a feeling.

This is why it's called a loop: we will continue to carry on the same patterns as before if we do not become aware of what thoughts we have on repeat. It isn't the divine-human in us we want to change; it's the thoughts that are making us unhappy with our lives and are stopping people from living life to their full potential.

You may be looking for the answer to how to start shifting these thoughts. Once you understand this loop, you can break limited beliefs, bad habits, and internal bullying.

In my world, a limited belief is a thought or assumption you've accepted as true about yourself or the world, but in fact, it's holding you back. It's like an invisible barrier stopping you from reaching your full potential. These beliefs often come from experiences or things people have said to us, and we start believing we're "not good enough," "not smart enough," or "not capable." But the truth is, they're just stories we tell ourselves; they are not facts.

Internal bullying is when you're harsh or critical toward yourself. It's that inner voice that says, "You can't do this," "You're going to fail," or "You're not as good as others." It's a form of self-sabotage that creates conflict within and makes it difficult to move forward with confidence. Just like any bully, this voice tries to keep you small.

Recognising it and challenging it is key to breaking free and growing.

Back to 'how' we break a limited belief.
You can break the loop at any point.
Let's say you want to start with thoughts, and the aim is to become aware and begin to catch yourself when you think of a limited, disempowering or negative thought.
If you thought,
"I'm never going to do that."
 You would acknowledge that statement and switch it to "I am going to do that".

A great tool I teach my clients is to write the statements down immediately. This way, you can see what thoughts you may be thinking unconsciously. Many start by changing their thoughts first, but it's not the easiest thing to do.

Changing your feelings first can also be tricky, as feelings are so connected to our thoughts, but remember, our thoughts are not us. Allowing our feelings to drive our vessel is a dangerous game, and many things in life wouldn't function. If I let my feelings drive me and make all my decisions, I would probably be lying on the sofa most days with a big tub of Ben and Jerry's vegan cookie dough ice cream, watching Gilmore Girls. Maybe you can relate. But I know those actions will not create success or inspire others to create their dream lives. If we allowed our feelings to control our everyday lives, we would get nothing done! Nothing in life would function the way it does. If you can find a way to change your feelings, then that's great, but I would suggest starting with action.

When I say action, I don't only mean the physical things you do; I also refer to the words you use out loud. Both doing something physical and speaking are both actions.

Remember when I said, 'Our thoughts create our reality'? This is exactly what I mean. When we start to speak different words, we begin to stop moaning so much and take full responsibility for everything in our lives. Our reality changes in such a profound way that it could easily be mistaken for magic.

Let's take a moment to see how changing our actions in language can help change the direction of the Thought Process Loop:

First, say out loud, "I am struggling." I am struggling. How did that make you feel?
Let's repeat it one more time with feeling… "I am struggling"…
Feels a bit sh*t, doesn't it? It feels heavy and low, physically and mentally.

Now, let's try a different approach. This time, say, "I am growing." I am growing.
How did that make you feel?
Let's say it again, but with feeling… "I am growing"…
Did you feel a difference, uplifting, hopeful and light?

Here's another example. Say the words "It's hard."
How did that make you feel?
Now, say, "I'm being challenged, and challenges help me progress."
How does that make you feel?
It's a bit more advanced, but you get the gist.

Hopefully, you can see that reframing your action in language has a hugely positive impact on how you feel, both emotionally and physically.

It's a loop, and everything is connected.

When you keep telling yourself, "I'm struggling", your brain believes it. It decides that whatever you're doing really is a struggle, which makes you feel bad and stressed. And because you feel so bad, you keep saying you're struggling. See what's happening? Your actions get stuck in this cycle, and you end up struggling even more.

Breaking the loop starts with shifting the words you say. Instead of focusing on the struggle, focus on the progress you can make and watch how quickly things start to shift. If you want to break the loop, start with small, physical actions.

For example, let's say you've always seen yourself as a lazy person; maybe others labelled you that way growing up, and now that voice is stuck in your head. Even when you try to shake it, the thought "I'm lazy" keeps creeping in.

Here's how to take action: When that voice pops up, do something small, like putting things away after you use them. It might seem insignificant, but it's not. Each time you follow through, you're showing yourself respect and proving that you can do what you set out to do.

As you keep taking those small actions, something shifts. You start seeing yourself differently, not as lazy but as someone who takes action. This new way of thinking makes you feel better about yourself, which fuels better habits and behaviours. This is how we break the patterns and rewire our subconscious by doing these practices consistently.

You don't have to fully believe it right away, but saying it out loud can help: "I'm someone who follows through."

As you can see, no matter where you start on the loop, thoughts, feelings, or actions changing one piece begin to shift the entire cycle. Feeling like you've hit a wall and everything sucks? I get it. Typically, we wallow, sit with the feeling and let it take over. That's exactly how I used to handle my bad days. My actions matched those disempowering thoughts, and guess what? That just turned the loop into a full-on wheel of misery.

But here's the game-changer: instead of letting the moment drag you down, you flip the script. Choose a new action, something empowering. Step outside, go for a walk, listen to something uplifting, or blast your favourite song and dance like a total weirdo.

Why? Because the choice is yours. You can stay stuck, or you can do something small to start shifting your energy. That one choice has the power to change everything.

I used to think someone would swoop in like a knight in shining armour and save me from the two-inch puddle I was drowning in, also known as my overthinking brain. But the older I got, the more I realised... no one was coming. The work had to start with me, and spoiler alert: it wasn't as dramatic as I thought. It was just about making small choices and actually sticking to them.

LIMITED BELIEFS

'Your only limits are those you set upon yourself.'

How we were conditioned by our parents and the people around us has limited our minds; once you become aware of this, you will start to notice it more.

Limitations are one of the main reasons we are unhappy. Our mind tells us we 'can't,' but our soul/spirit knows we can, and this causes a conflict within ourselves. Let me explain that a little more: the soul/spirit is the thing that creates who we truly are, our authentic selves. Our authentic self has no limitations. It believes in us more than anyone.

But our mind has other plans. Our minds create problems, and usually, problems that are not real or factual. We can compare ourselves with others and listen to others' negative thoughts and beliefs. This is why we feel so much conflict: half of us know we can, but the other half is scared.

But the thing is, we always have choices, whether to choose disempowering or empowering beliefs.
Our subconscious mind can't invent new information. It can only work with what it already knows. Sometimes, we act like we've got it all figured out, but really, everything we think we know is based on what we've already learned. This becomes our perspective on the world and our lives.

If you were told that earning money had to be hard, even if you like your job, your mind would likely focus on all the tricky bits of the job, or because someone conditioned you to think earning was hard, you don't do it at all. Because the fear of the mind and the belief can take over.

Getting money does not have to be challenging, but many people, like my family, told me, 'You must work hard if you want a good life.' The fact is, that is as true as you want it to be. I love my mum; she is one of the most hardworking humans I've ever met.

When I was growing up, she had 7 jobs... I'm not kidding. She then started working for the NHS and built herself up to work multiple positions in the surgery. No one is as hardworking as my mum; she comes home after a hard day and cares for my nan; the woman is a superhuman. But does she make more money than others, even though she works longer and harder...? Hell no!

Heard of the saying, 'Work smart, not hard'? Even though I wasn't raised in an environment where people spoke or acted this way, I reconditioned myself to believe that 'earning money is not hard.' It's about having a system that works.

Did you know that 70-80% of our thoughts are repetitive thoughts from yesterday, last week, last month, or even our whole lives?

Now that you've started going inward and learning how to communicate with yourself, it's time to put those thoughts on paper. Pull them apart in your journal and begin to break down those limiting beliefs."

Journalling where this limited statement has come from is a great way to uncover these beliefs; as you know, the unconscious mind cannot create new information. An experience must happen, or the people around you, even the TV you watch, has limited you. It's important to figure out where this limitation comes from. Maybe you can hear one of your family members' voices in your head when this statement pops up. Start to remember the earliest time you heard your limited statement.

So, if these limited beliefs have been installed by others externally, surely they can be uninstalled from within? Yes!

Example Belief:

'Earning money is hard work.'

Take a moment to reflect and challenge your belief with the following questions:

- Why do I believe this?

- Why does it have to be hard?

- Who told me this?

- When was the last time I heard this statement?

- Why does this feel true to me?

- Is this 100% a fact?

- Have there been times in my life when earning money felt easy?

By breaking this belief down, you can begin to uncover its roots and decide whether it still serves you. Remember, beliefs are not facts. They're thoughts we've accepted as truth over time.

Then, ask, "If money wasn't hard, what would it look like?" Start to come up with 3-4 ways to make money more easily. Now that you have journaled this out a bit, you will notice it when you say it next.

This would be the same process for any limited beliefs; it's about questioning and challenging the belief to find out where it came from and pulling it apart to prove it's a belief rather than a fact. This could be the same for believing you are not good enough or can not achieve what you desire.

I've made this diagram to help you see how the pattern of disempowering and empowering forms. You can even write these questions out for your limiting beliefs. Seeing your thoughts on paper can make it much easier to break them down and shift your mindset.

LIMITED BELIEF

DISEMPOWERING

EMPOWERING

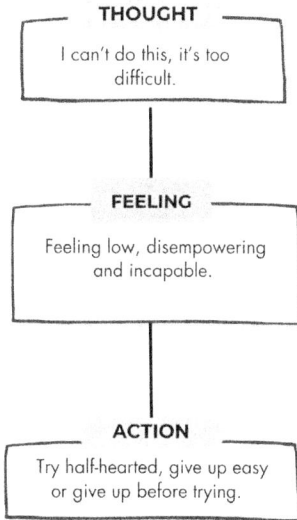

THOUGHT

I can't do this, it's too difficult.

FEELING

Feeling low, disempowering and incapable.

ACTION

Try half-hearted, give up easy or give up before trying.

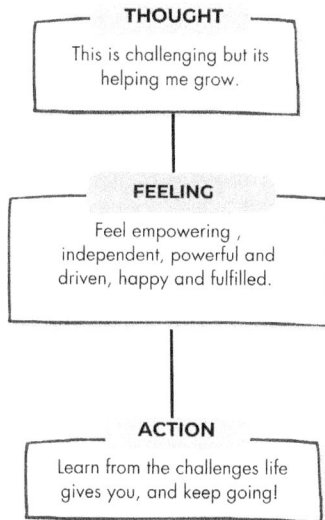

THOUGHT

This is challenging but its helping me grow.

FEELING

Feel empowering, independent, powerful and driven, happy and fulfilled.

ACTION

Learn from the challenges life gives you, and keep going!

OUR THOUGHTS ARE NOT US

'Living in your head too much = anxiety.'

I never listened to and absorbed this information at my lowest; I would hear but never listen. I was in what we call a 'fixed' mindset. I believed, due to my conditioning, that I would and could never change, and this is precisely what a fixed mindset means: that you are unable to see that you can make changes when you start making different decisions.

If you, like I used to, suffer from overthinking syndrome, then listen up!

Take a moment to think about the clouds that pass above us. They are just clouds; they can't help the shapes they form into. Our thoughts are the same. They move and reshape as fast as we figure out what they actually are. We don't blame the clouds for making certain shapes. So why do we blame ourselves for thinking certain thoughts? Once we understand and fully accept that we are not our thoughts, we can move on in our journey because analysing every thought we have wastes so much energy and steals our happiness.

This takes us to be fully present in the moment because when we are fully present in the moment, our anxiety, depression and stress fizzle away (unless you are in a life-or-death situation or a serious event has happened in the present moment).

In this day and age, we can make a lot of excuses for why we don't want to heal or become better because staying the same becomes our comfort; the change which is needed for growth affects our comfort and 'safety' zone. We forget that many of our ancestors were victims of wars, homelessness, being extremely poor and being forced to stay in survival mode even from thousands of years before our Grandparents. We forget that we are living and not just surviving because of our ancestors and how they lived; this energy and way of being has been passed down. Their pain, trauma, worries, and anxiety from living in these conditions have affected our vibration. But waking up from this is one of the key ways to truly find happiness and freedom; we should be so grateful.

Now that I've planted that seed, let's throw in a tool to help.

Choose a calming song; it could be anything. There is no wrong or right. What you feel is calming for you. Set a one-minute timer, get comfortable, close your eyes, and focus on breathing until your alarm goes off. If you think a thought, accept it, let it float away and carry on focusing on your breath. See your thoughts as passing without any judgment.

This is a form of meditation which is not only good for reducing stress, improving focus, and enhancing emotional balance but also boosts overall physical and mental health by calming the nervous system, lowering cortisol, and increasing oxygen flow to the brain.

Some people like to brush this exercise off. You might say, 'It's not my thing,' which is fine, as we are all different, and different things work for different people. But I must say, breathing exercises work, and mediations work!

The same principle applies to fruits and vegetables; some people may not like eating them, but it doesn't make them less healthy. It's so easy to make a million excuses to get out of your comfort zone, and humans can be compulsive excuse-makers; I know, I was one of them. But letting go of all excuses, even if there is an actual valid excuse, is a massive burden off your shoulders.

Stop making excuses by reminding yourself that you deserve to show up for you. When you notice an excuse creeping in, even if it feels valid, gently call yourself out. Say, "I've got this," or "I'm doing this because it matters to me." Be kind, but stay accountable. Flip the script, and start proving to yourself that you can.

If and when you think of a questionable thought, maybe it's a negative comment about yourself or someone else or just a straight-up WEIRD thought. I want you to tell yourself, 'My thoughts are not me.' and simply laugh the thought off. Then tell yourself, "I am in control of what thoughts I focus on, and I only choose to focus on happy, motivating and inspiring thoughts." That's it… Don't analyse, overthink or worry. Don't worry if you find this hard. Over time and with consistency, it will get easier, I promise!

As I said in the first chapter, we have around 80,000 thoughts per day, and if we start to assume that the thoughts we think are who we are and let them define us, we will become emotional wrecks and compulsive overthinkers like I used to be. Analysing everything, every pattern will make you go crazy; our job is to observe them. If you don't like a thought, that's fine; tell yourself that thought does not resonate with the person you are; letting it go and moving on is the most important thing you can do.

A lot of people come to me struggling with anxiety, so let's talk about it and make it a little less scary. Anxiety is a normal human emotion rooted in our fight-or-flight response. It's your brain trying to protect you. Think of it like a squad of tiny soldiers, hard-wired to keep you safe. But sometimes, those soldiers overreact and sound the alarm when there's no real danger.

When they do, your body releases stress hormones like cortisol and adrenaline, triggering symptoms like a racing heart, rapid breathing, muscle tension, sweating, or even headaches. It's your body gearing up for action, even if you don't need it.

Here's the thing: anxiety is normal, and it's trying to help you. But if it's starting to run your life, try this mantra: "Thank you, anxiety, for trying to keep me safe, but I do not give you permission to take over my life." It's a small step, but it can make a big difference in calming those overactive soldiers.

 Another way to look at it is that anxiety is energy and can be very powerful when choosing to use that energy for empowering actions and thoughts. I say embrace that fear and turn it into a pure, powerful passion. Anxiety comes from *overthinking about the past and worrying about the future*. When you are in the present moment, this eliminates anxiety unless you are in a life-or-death situation. The best choice is to step out of your mind and pull the **facts** apart from the **feeling.** Let me break that down for you. When experiencing anxiety, it's important to separate the fact (the actual situation) from the feeling (the emotional reaction) to gain clarity and control.

Anxiety - thinking about the past and worrying about the future. Stay in the present to avoid anxiety.

Anxiety often traps us in a reactive state, clouding our perception and keeping us stuck in survival mode. To break free, we must explore the three levels of consciousness, which reveal how our mind operates and where we can reclaim control.

As I mentioned earlier, when we have a basic understanding of how and why things work, it becomes easier to create long-lasting results. So, I thought I'd take a moment to explain the three levels of consciousness to give you a clearer understanding of how the mind functions.

Conscious Mind

Our minds are pretty incredible, aren't they? Here's a fun fact: we only use a tiny fraction of their full potential! Let's talk about the three levels of consciousness, starting with the **Conscious Mind**:

- **What it is**: The conscious mind is basically everything you're aware of at the moment: your thoughts, feelings, and whatever's happening right now.
- **What it does**: This is where all your logical thinking, decision-making, and "get-it-done" energy lives. It's what helps you handle your day-to-day tasks and stay tuned in to the world around you.
- **For example**: Anytime you're planning your day, having a chat, or deciding what to eat, you're working in your conscious mind. Simple as that!

Let's keep going. It gets even better!

Subconscious (or Unconscious) Mind

Now, let's dive a little deeper. The **Subconscious Mind** is where the magic happens behind the scenes.

- **What it is**: Think of it as the storage room of your mind. It holds all the stuff you're not actively thinking about right now, memories, past experiences, and everything you've learned, ready to pop up when needed.
- **What it does**: It's the boss of all the automatic stuff, like keeping you breathing, digesting, and fighting off

colds. But it's also where your beliefs, habits, and emotions live, quietly shaping how you think, feel, and act without you even realising it.

- **For example**: Have you ever driven somewhere familiar and realised you barely remember the trip? Or did you feel an emotional reaction to something that reminded you of an old experience? That's your subconscious mind doing its thing.

It's like the autopilot of your life, always working, even when you're not paying attention!

Superconscious Mind
Now we're getting to the really fascinating stuff, the **Superconscious Mind**, the part that feels like it's connected to something bigger than us.

- **What it is**: This is the higher level of your mind, where you tap into universal wisdom, creativity, and spiritual insight. It's like the bridge between you and the infinite, giving you access to something beyond everyday thought.
- **What it does**: The superconscious mind helps you see the bigger picture, sparking those "aha!" moments, deep spiritual connections, and creative breakthroughs. It's where you access your intuition and those profound feelings of unity with the world around you.

- **An example**: Have you ever had a sudden burst of inspiration out of nowhere, felt deeply connected during meditation, or had a moment of clarity that felt almost divine? That's your superconscious mind at work. It's the part of your mind that reminds you there's more to life than what we see on the surface.

The superconscious is the all-knowing. When you start tapping into yourself and practising what I have taught you in this book, you will start to become aware of it.

An example was when I was stuck in a traffic jam and was on my phone to check directions (my car was not moving). In the back of my head, I thought, what if someone had a camera recording me? Being on your phone in the UK with your engine on is illegal, even if you are not moving. I looked up and to my right, and yes… there was a man filming me. There was no way I could have seen him out of the corner of my eye, but my higher self, my superconscious, the all-knowing part of myself, knew that there was someone filming me.

When you begin to understand that we are all connected and you have gone through all the stages of healing and the life-changing events that happen in your life, that is when the awakening begins.

THE REFLECTION THEORY

∽

"As the saying goes, 'Everything is a reflection of one's self.'"

I remember when I was younger, my relationship with my family wasn't the best. I never understood why everyone always seemed so angry or upset. Looking back, I get it now. But back then, I took every bit of anger, every argument, every moment of sadness so personally. If someone raised their voice, I'd burst into tears or snap back, mirroring the same energy right back at them.

But here's the thing: this chapter isn't about reflecting other people's emotions. It's about how we see the world and how it reflects back at us. Our perspective shapes our reality. Once I understood that, I realised I wasn't just responding to others; I was creating my own experience. It was a game-changer. When I shifted my view, everything else followed. Life started looking a whole lot brighter, and I found the power to change the story that I was living.

The reflection theory is the key to most of your problems. ' I come from a generation that wants the last word, is impatient, and gets offended easily. I know why; no one has explained the reflection theory to them! I hope this helps.

Okay, let's consider this: When someone is self-conscious about their appearance, they may unconsciously project their insecurities onto others by commenting on other people's bodies, whether to their face, behind their back, or even just in their thoughts. When someone criticises you, and you know that you didn't do anything to deserve it, remind yourself it's a reflection of that person. It means that how people react to things often reflects their own emotions or insecurities rather than the true meaning of what was said.

For example, suppose someone says something neutral to another, and they get upset. In that case, it's usually because of that person's own feelings or experiences, not because the comment was intended to hurt them. Their reaction says more about what's going on with them internally. We can get so emotionally attached to people's reasons, but understanding this simple psychology helps you to take your emotions out of it.

When people are always angry, such as a family member who regularly speaks to you disrespectfully, it's because they are holding onto something; this means they are unhappy. The only reason they are shouting and screaming and feel it's acceptable to speak to you in that way is because they speak to themselves in that way. This is what makes them think that they can talk to you in the same way as they speak to themselves.

For example, let's say someone is trying to explain something to you, and they start shouting. You ask, "Why are you shouting?" Their response is something like: "It's because this is the only way I can get through to you, the only way you'll listen."

There are two ways to look at this:

One, they're being a complete d*ck… (Just kidding, but seriously, not cool.)

Or, two, they shout and scream at themselves, so they think this is the only way to get through to anyone. They treat themselves like sh*t, and disrespect themselves daily, so it seems 'normal' to take that out on others.

They haven't dealt with their own demons. Maybe they were shouted at as kids, disrespected, or scared into submission, and they've never broken that generational trauma. This is the cycle they're stuck in, and it reflects how they've been taught to communicate. It's not about you; it's about them and where they've come from.

This is why it's so important not to take ANYTHING personally, even if it is an attack against you. Do not allow anyone to affect your energy, happiness or love, even your family.

I will give a real-life example of how I realised this: When I was neck-deep in one of my first businesses, like I said before, I knew this company and industry was not for me, but at the same time, so I was unaware. I kept looking for the answer. I would say, 'Universe, give me a sign, tell me what I should be doing... why do I feel so incomplete?'. Little did I know the answer was in the questions I asked other's . I know it sounds weird!

I always asked my partner, "Are you sure you're happy in your business? Are you sure it's your passion?"Of course, his answer was yes. I would ask my mum the same questions over and over again like a broken record. I hope you can see where I'm going with this! I would say this stuff on repeat because the company I was building just wasn't right for me.

When I finally realised that this was the universe's sign, this is why I personally believe God, Mother Nature, or the universe lies within us. We have ALL THE ANSWERS we need, all within us. Looking out for the signs within is always the answer we need.

When we understand, embody, and acknowledge that everyone is a reflection of themself, we can finally let go of the comments people make about us, the abuse we receive, the hate we feel, and the hate we feel toward others or even ourselves. You finally get to let go because you now understand that if someone is rude, judgmental, or hurtful, you don't have to be offended because you know it has nothing to do with you. The same goes for when you are rude, judgmental, or nasty about others or yourself; you can now look within and ask why.

Start to become aware of what things annoy you in others; this is usually an indication of some emotion that you have not healed or looked over yet. Start to become aware, and everything will start to flow. Healing becomes natural and second nature when you start to learn more about how we humans function.

It's easy to overanalyse this, but most of the time, it's a reflection of self. When people overanalyse others and pick others' behaviours and actions apart, this usually happens because they are unhappy. If you find yourself in this situation, remind yourself to focus on your journey, your own path.

Have you ever been in a situation where someone's comment made you feel angry and unsettled even when you knew their comment wasn't about you or even offended you? Yet here you are, letting your emotions take over your life.

What do we call this? A trigger! Yes, who has been triggered or has triggers that come up multiple times?

TRIGGERS

'As the saying goes, let your triggers be your guide.'

Our triggers come from our conditioning, something we will go through in the next chapter; we get triggered when a situation arises that either makes us uncomfortable, upset, angry or scared. These, too, can come from traumatic experiences.

When a triggering situation comes up, most people like to sweep it under the rug and by this, I mean they try their very best to control situations around them to avoid being triggered. I am not here to tell you exactly what to do with your life, but hiding from the situation or controlling outcomes in life, in general, is a toxic, unnatural thing to do in the long run. Because the triggers aren't just popping up to say 'Hey!' they are coming to be let go, but it's sometimes easier to control the situation by pushing it down and avoiding them altogether.

If you want to set yourself free from your triggers, it's important to face them. Once a triggering event has happened, dig deep. Ask yourself, 'Why?' "Why has this event triggered me?" Does it have to do with a situation that occurred when you were a child, or does it remind you of an embarrassing moment? Most of the time, it's a little deeper than the eye meets; we can understand where it has come from by facing it.

Once you have worked out where it comes from, you will start to understand that you are not upset with the person who triggered you; the trigger lies deep within, and that's why it's called a TRIGGER, as it only takes something or someone to say or do something to let it rip.

For me, my trigger was people shouting at me; I would get upset, and my chest would get incredibly tight. Still, to this day, I feel some sort of tightness in my chest when people raise their voices. My breathing would speed up, and I would feel like crying; I understand this came from my childhood, but even though I KNEW where it was coming from, I still 'couldn't' shift it. It was affecting my relationships with people. They wouldn't even have to shout at me for me to feel that. It could have been someone speaking sternly, not because they were angry or annoyed, simply because that is how they spoke.

I had this one life coach for a short amount of time. His coaching style wasn't for me, so it didn't last long. However, I am grateful for the two pieces of information he gave me. He asked, "Do you think these people are trying to hurt you?" After reflecting, I realised they weren't trying to hurt me; they were just being themselves.

That was the key! It helped me move on from being triggered to not allowing it to affect me and my relationships. It was that simple... asking myself, "Was this person trying to hurt me?" Questions are so powerful.

I wish I could say this method worked immediately, but we humans are conditioned, and it takes time, consistency, and practice. I want to remind you that as a human, methods, tools, and practices are not perfected overnight (whatever "perfect" is).

I can't express enough the power of acknowledgment; acknowledging when you are being triggered allows you to understand better and heal yourself, and it also helps you create better relationships with the people around you.

When you feel triggered, whip out your journal or phone and write down what triggered you. Then, journal on it and start digging for the root. Where did that trigger come from?

Allowing yourself to be open and honest and asking the questions that will help you release past stress or traumas will not only help you feel lighter within your mind, but you, too, will feel the lightness in your physical body!

A great tool to use to help you when you have found the root cause of your trigger is, every time it comes up, to think of this past experience and go back to the 'How To Let The F*ck Go' Chapter and do the letting go steps I taught you.

MISERY LOVES COMPANY

Have you heard of the saying 'Misery loves company'?

During the beginning of your awakening to this new perspective of life, you will start to notice the negative entities that people have attached to themselves. You'll begin to notice the negative energy that some people carry around with them. It's like they're carrying emotional baggage that impacts their attitude, actions, or the way they treat others. You can see it in their reactions, their outlook, and even in the way they speak.

Recognising these 'negative entities' helps you understand that this energy isn't yours to take on. It's just something they're carrying. When you become aware of it, you can set boundaries and protect your energy.

You will start to see life differently. This also means seeing people in other lights. This is no time for judgment, hate, or justification. Everyone is on their own journey, and as much as we want them to see the light that we now see in the world, making them feel bad, stressed, or wrong will not help anyone; it will create stress for them. Trust me, I tried this approach, which wastes energy.

In many teachings, I've learned that leading by example is the best way to handle these situations. Like I said before, people around you will notice differences in you. Your job is not to 'teach' them the way but to lead by example and offer small guidance if they ask.

I will refer back to the quote, 'Misery loves company.' When people are unhappy, many do not want someone trying to lift them and raise their vibration; they want to bring you down to the same level. Once you see this, you can start taking action to protect your energy. When you see this happen, changing the subject or walking away is essential. People may think I am rude when I shut off from a negative conversation or situation, but I truly and honestly do not care what they think.

If I allow someone's negative or disempowering energy to affect my mind, it brings me *DOWN*. Like many others, I am an empath, which means you can feel people's emotions/energy/frequency without even speaking to them. When people open up to empaths, they feel the same feelings as the person struggling. I've done enough work to put a barrier up, but sometimes, some energy will get through, leaving me feeling drained. There is a difference between someone wanting genuine help and guidance and another wanting to lower your vibration.

You may find people dropping out of your life during this time. The reason is that we attract what we give out; if you have been vibrating on a self-pity, sad, angry, or disempowering level, you will have attracted those people into your life. Or you have had those people in your life since you were younger. You, too, will see these people in another way.

You may not feel the same way about these people, but try to remember that they, too, have been conditioned, and we are all doing our best with the knowledge and things we have. Like I said before, this is no time to judge them; lift your energy and send them love, and your light and energy will become infectious.

I used to dislike it when people told me to "send love" to those who had hurt, upset, or disrespected me but hear me out. We now understand that everyone is a reflection of themselves, so when people say hurtful things to you, it's because that's how they feel. When they speak disrespectfully, it's a reflection of how they speak to themselves. When they behave hurtfully, it's a reflection of their pain.

There's no benefit in holding onto anger and taking it personally. Instead, feel sorry for them and send them as much love as possible, and then you can move forward.

You are not stooping down to their level; you are simply being the kind and loving person you are. If you act the same as them and mirror their behaviour, then you will stoop down to their level. Before I started to see this, I used to think that if someone treated me a certain way, I would mirror their actions and behaviours. If someone did not respect me, I wouldn't respect them. If someone is going to be rude to me, you guessed it, I was going to do the same back.

But can you see what's happening? It's like the other person throwing a ball of fire at you, then you catch it and throw it back. What a waste of your time and energy. Not only do you get hit by the fire, but you're also holding it, getting burnt! This is the same teaching from Buddhist teaching:

'Holding on to anger is like grasping a hot coal with the intent of throwing it at someone else; you are the one who gets burned.'
-Buddha

By continuing to be your loving self and not fighting fire with fire, you are simply dodging the fire through the protection you have around you and sending them what is in your soul: love.

I don't mean you should say kind things and say you love them; you can do this, but I mean sending them more energetic love. You can do whatever feels right to you, as there are no wrongs and rights, but in my many years of being around explosive and negative people, this is the best way I've dealt with them.

This is truly beautiful, not allowing people to f*ck up and unravel all the self-development work you have done.

The choice is yours to choose love and understanding.

UNCONSCIOUSLY CONDITIONED

'Being human means having the ability to be conditioned, but also the power to break free from those conditions.'

Learning this shifted me from a victim mindset to an empowered mentality. For years, I thought I was broken. I'd snap at the smallest thing or feel hurt in a millisecond, all because of emotions I hadn't dealt with. Honestly, I put a lot of the blame on my family. It wasn't about trying to feel better by blaming them; it was just that I knew, deep down, that their traumas and pain had seeped into me, shaping my thoughts and reactions.

I'd learned about default energy, and I could see how certain events and energies from my childhood, even from before I was born, had impacted me mentally and physically (stress really does live in the body).

There's a great book on this: The Body Keeps the Score by Bessel van der Kolk.

But there was something I was missing: accountability. I realised I had to own my conditioning. Yes, those experiences shaped me, but I also had a choice. I could keep replaying the blame game, or I could start the work of rewiring my mind. And you can guess what I chose.

This decision transformed me from being a victim of my circumstances to someone who owns, learns, and grows from them. It's helped me break old patterns and, in turn, support others on their journeys. It's powerful what taking accountability can do. It's a whole new level of freedom

'The same event happens, but there are two points of view.'
We are all conditioned by a few key factors in our lives, especially when we're young.

Between the ages of 1 and 7, our minds are like sponges, soaking up not only the words spoken but also the energy people around us give off. So, we naturally absorb and feel the things people say and the emotions they express. This creates and plays a part in our default energy.

For example, if everyone around you constantly screamed, shouted, and were stressed out during this time, you would have taken all that in. The same goes if you were surrounded by calmness, love, and respect; you'd have absorbed that same energy, too. You pick up the energy around you at such a young age!

Age 1-7 = feeling the same energy, vibe, and frequency as those around you.

From the ages of 7 to 14, you enter your modelling stage, where you begin to mimic and mirror the behaviours of those around you consciously. During this time, you're not just observing; you're actively learning how to respond to the world. If the people around you express their anger through violence, you're likely to model that behaviour, believing that's how conflicts should be handled. On the other hand, if you see people around you meditating or calming things down when situations get intense, you'll model that approach instead.

It's not just about their actions, the words they use, the choices they make, and the energy they give off. You absorb it all. Whether healthy or unhealthy, you take in those cues and mirror them, shaping your behaviours, attitudes, and ways of dealing with the world. Essentially, you become a reflection of your environment during these crucial years, carrying those modelled behaviours into adulthood unless you consciously break the cycle.

Age 7-14 = mimicking the same physical actions as the others around you and feeling their energy.

Between the ages of 14 and 21, the influence of friends plays a major role in shaping your behaviour, habits, and even identity. During this time, you're highly impressionable, and your peer group becomes a powerful force in your life. If your friends smoke or engage in risky behaviours, you might feel pressure to follow suit, even if it goes against your values. Similarly, if they disrespected their parents, you could mimic that behaviour, thinking it's normal or 'cool'.

On the flip side, this influence can also work in positive ways. If your friends were passionate about music, art, or sports, you might develop a similar interest. You'll likely adopt their hobbies, tastes, and even ways of thinking. Whether it's how they talk, dress, or handle challenges, you're continuously shaped by their influence, sometimes consciously, but often without even realising it. This stage is all about figuring out where you fit in and who you want to become, and your friends play a big part in that process.

Age 14-21 = The same as above, but observing and modelling friends. No, this doesn't always happen like this, but you get my drift.

Once you hit **21** and beyond, your career path starts to seriously reshape your life, your beliefs, and how you show up in the world. The experiences you go through in your work life begin to influence how you see yourself, what you value, and what you believe you're capable of achieving.

Your career choices impact everything, from how you spend your time, the people you surround yourself with, and even your lifestyle. Whether chasing that corporate ladder, building your own business, or going after something creative, your career becomes a key part of your identity. You'll start developing new habits and behaviours based on your job's demands and the professional culture around you. Every decision, every relationship, and how you handle success or setbacks all start to shape the way you see the world.

Plus, your sense of purpose sharpens as your career evolves. You begin to align your values with your professional goals, looking for fulfilment not just through money but through meaningful work that makes a difference.

The choices you make in your 20s and beyond lay the foundation for your future, redefining who you are and how you engage with the world.

Have you ever heard the saying, "You can't teach an old dog new tricks?" Well, neuroscientists have thoroughly debunked that! You *can absolutely* recondition yourself with the right mix of Consistency, Repetition, Accountability, and Knowledge. This is how real, long-lasting change happens, and I've seen it time and time again.

The belief that you can't change is a limitation you put on yourself. When you understand that your patterns and habits can shift with the power of your mind, you'll see why these principles are so important:

Consistency: You've been conditioned a certain way your whole life, so it's unrealistic to think you'll undo years of conditioning in just a month. Real change takes consistent effort. Show up for yourself every single day.

Repetition: Change comes from doing the work repeatedly, using the same tools, practising the same exercises, and learning and re-learning the same lessons. Over time, this repetition rewires your brain to create lasting transformation.

Accountability: No one can do the work for you. You are the one who has the power to change your behaviours and habits. Hold yourself accountable for your growth, and take ownership of your journey.

Transformation is 100% possible when you embrace these principles. It's not a quick fix, but with dedication, you can recondition your mind and create your desired life.

Each of us has been conditioned, and it is clear to see when two people have been conditioned differently. The same events happen in both people's lives, yet their reactions are miles apart. Is there a right way or a wrong way? No, there isn't; it's just two different ways of thinking that have been altered by conditioning. Once you understand and accept that different aspects of your life have conditioned you, you can start to change it.

Personally, before I understood the knowledge behind human conditioning, I would play the victim. Not badly and not out loud, but to myself. I made up excuses for why I was acting the way I was. Don't get me wrong; I had a valid point. I acted up and got triggered by situations, and there was a reason for my behaviour.

The way I was thinking and acting was due to my conditioning; I had a choice to recondition myself, but because I didn't have the knowledge behind why or how, I was stuck in an unconscious conditioning loop that I was somewhat blind to! I was playing the victim even though I had no idea I was doing it.

When I learnt I had been in victim mode this whole time, the first thing that came to me was… "Back then, I was too *young, dumb and depressed* to understand this beautiful concept, but now... now I am an adult. I can decide to change and reshape my mind the way I want to be and live."

Right now, you have the basic knowledge behind why you react, why you think certain things, why you feel certain emotions or say certain things... You can let go of making up excuses for yourself. We have all been conditioned, and if we all made up excuses for our behaviours, then no one would grow, and no one would take full responsibility for their lives. We would live in a world of victimising ourselves; we would all become slaves to our past.

I hear many people say they 'can't' or make statements about how they are 'broken' and no one can fix them. Only half of that statement is correct; no one can truly 'fix' you but you. But... what even is broken? What defines broken? Just because you went through sh*t, that doesn't mean to say you let those past experiences define you and become your identity. That was one of the limited statements I had in my mind for many years. What makes broken, and what makes fixed? What do these words even mean? Any meaning we give them.

The difference between then (when I felt broken) and now is that I've built a relationship with myself. I've taken the time to get to know myself, and most importantly, I ask myself questions.

For example, let's say I get offended by something a family member says. Instead of just reacting, I'll write down a simple question like, "Why did you react that way?" or "Why did this statement upset or trigger you?" From there, I have an open conversation with myself, digging deeper into my emotions and thoughts to get to the root of the issue. This process often takes consistency and repetition, just like I mentioned earlier. The more I practise it, the clearer my understanding becomes, and that's where real healing begins.

It's about being honest with myself, allowing space to explore what's going on in my head, and taking responsibility for my reactions.

How interesting is this? We have been conditioned, so we most likely believed what our parents said to us. As I mentioned in an earlier chapter, "Talking to yourself is the first sign of madness."

Who's heard of that saying? Who was brought up hearing and being told this? I was! You know what, when I was younger, every time I would speak to myself, I honestly thought I needed to go to a therapist or be put in a psychiatric hospital (I wish I was kidding, I can laugh about it now).

Most of us have been conditioned to think like everyone else and to say what the majority says. We have been conditioned by what other people in different generations have taught us, and now we know that speaking with yourself is one of the best things you can do!

You can recondition your thought process... the things I've taught you in this book will reshape and recondition you, but the work is done within your inner self.

ACCOUNTABILITY

'Holding yourself fully accountable: cause and effect.'

Do you take full responsibility for everything in your life?

Let's put that to the test, shall we?

If you are truly ready and committed to making positive and long-lasting changes, it's time to hold yourself fully accountable for everything... You heard me, *everything*! Like running late, not paying a bill on time, forgetting something, or waking up late.

I know, scary, right?

There is no proof that everything in your life is entirely your 'fault', but it's only when we change from blame to accountability that we hold the power of our own lives in our hands. This theory is called *cause* and *effect* or the *Feedback Loop*

Cause – Focusing on the results (fixing the 'problem').
Effect – Focusing on the reasons (making excuses or finding reasons why you haven't).

When we blame other people or situations, we're handing over our power. It's like saying, "This is out of my control," which leaves us stuck and frustrated. But the second we stop pointing fingers and start looking at what *we* can change, we take that power back. We stop being victims of life and start actually living it on our terms.

Empowering is taking full responsibility for everything in our lives, and disempowering is blaming and making excuses for everything in our lives.

For example, I needed a key cut, but it wasn't straightforward because it was a Chinese-made key. Most shops couldn't do it, but one guy said he could and told me to come down to his shop. So, an hour or two later, I drove all the way there... and it was closed.

Now, the old me, the unaccountable me, would've been stressed and angry. I'd have blamed the guy for not telling me when they closed and probably called my partner to have a massive rant about it.

But you know what I did instead? I laughed. I thought, "I should've checked their opening times online." And just like that, the stress was gone. Owning it felt so much better than blaming someone else. It was such a small moment, but it showed me how powerful it is to put the responsibility back on myself.

I'd like you to start implementing accountability into your life. Next time you are late for something and want to blame the traffic, hold your hands up and say, "Sorry, I'm late." End of story. No excuses, blame yourself, laugh it off, and learn from your mistakes. Trust me, it will make you feel a lot better! If you are feeling triggered, GOOD! I'm glad, as you now know, our triggers indicate things we can work on; remember the saying 'let your triggers be your guides'.

As I said right at the beginning of the book, the aim isn't to always be perfect. It's simply *acknowledging* and becoming aware of when you are, in effect, making excuses for your life and changing that to 'cause' fixing the problem.

I am not implying that if something horrific happened to you, you should blame yourself. I am coming at this from a lighter, day-to-day perspective. However, remembering everything that happens to us shapes who we are. Scars build our character, strengthen us, and open our eyes to different ways of thinking and seeing the world. It's your choice to see it from an empowering or disempowering perspective.

We are like plants; when rain comes down, it helps the plants grow, and this is the same for us humans. How will we grow if only 'good' things happen to us? Challenges, trauma, and resistance also create growth and form new, more open perceptions of the world. When you start to see the pain and suffering you have endured in your life more like this, this creates a 'growth mindset. ' When you have a growth mindset, you are truly unstoppable. This is where the saying *mind over matter* comes from. We can choose to let past experiences either define us or make us stronger. Your mindset may have been conditioned, but it's your choice to rewire that conditioning.

When I started to hold myself fully accountable for everything in my life, it became easier to detach myself from my past traumas, triggers and the physical pain I felt from my childhood. I realised that I had a choice. I could choose to let my past define me, depress me, drag me down, and destroy me for the rest of my life.

Alternatively, I could understand that I have been conditioned this way and make the choice to recondition myself, taking full responsibility for my actions, the words I use, and the thoughts I think. Once you do this, you will be freed from the past weighing heavily on your shoulders.

KNOWING YOUR VALUES

'Not knowing your core values is like trying to play darts blindfolded. How are you supposed to hit the target if you don't even know where it is?'

Before I sat and communicated with myself daily, I was throwing darts left, right, and definitely not centre for years!

I've discussed this before in previous chapters, but due to my lack of communication with myself, I fell down a rabbit hole, building a business and life that was so far from my values and morals.

Our whole lives are based on the decisions we make. But if you don't know your values, how can you possibly make decisions that lead to real happiness? Your values are your guide. Without them, you're just reacting to life instead of intentionally choosing what's best for your growth and fulfilment. When you know your values, you can make choices that align with the life you truly want! Our whole lives are based on the decisions we make.

Let me say that again…

OUR WHOLE LIVES ARE BASED ON THE DECISIONS WE MAKE.

When you have not worked out your values in life, how on earth are you meant to make decisions that will benefit you and make you happy?

Looking at your life right now, can you say you are happy?
If you answered that question with a no, ask yourself this question:
Do you know your core values?

Example of values:
- **Spending time with family**: If this is a core value for you, going to the pub every night and leaving your family at home wouldn't align with what you truly care about.
- **Freedom**: If freedom is one of your values, taking a job that restricts your choices or being with a partner who limits your freedom would conflict with that.
- **Health**: If you value health, eating fast food regularly wouldn't line up with your desire to live a healthy lifestyle.
- **Animal rights**: If you value animal rights, supporting industries like animal testing or the meat and dairy industries wouldn't be in line with your beliefs.

Knowing your values helps you live with more intention and stay true to what really matters to you. If you know your core values, ask yourself. Do you make decisions based on them?

For example, one of my values is freedom, as choosing to build a brick-and-mortar service business didn't align with my values. Another of my values is animal rights, so deciding to train to become an aesthetics practitioner was far from my values and morals.

When I started learning this, my life changed... and fast! I started to make decisions based only on what I wanted and what truly aligned with the true me, not just 'social media happiness' or 'population happiness. '

Once we change our perception, when I tell you, our whole life changes, everything we see is in a new light, a new colour. It is only when you start making decisions based on your morals and values that the world, only then the world is truly yours.

Align your values with your whole life, relationships, job, home, and purpose to unlock everything you have always wanted.

One modern-day issue that affects our decision-making is that we live in a world with too many choices. Which, in some aspects, could be considered a great thing. However, I'm not saying it isn't. But some people now have developed *shiny object syndrome*. This means a tendency to be easily distracted by new or exciting opportunities, ideas, or objects and having difficulty staying focused on one task or goal. Now more than ever, it is easy to look to the outer world to find purpose for the things that will bring them fulfilment. Instead of staying true to who you are, what you like, what you are good at, and what you enjoy. Social media, the internet, and the news distract us from our purpose.

Let's imagine you've noticed several individuals making money from stocks. You see the freedom they have, travelling to beautiful countries, working remotely, and you start to think, "That's what I want." So, you start buying stock courses, watching YouTube videos on stock investing, and dedicating much time to it.

However, you soon realise that the effort and knowledge required to become as successful as those you've seen on social media doesn't bring you happiness. The process stresses you out and fails to provide fulfilment. Then, you notice a few individuals on social media who have started their own service businesses. They talk about their earnings and how easy it is, so you sign up for their training course. Yet again, you find yourself discontented because you dislike providing the service and dealing with long hours of clients. It becomes clear that your choices are not fulfilling because they are based on other people's success or happiness, and you are simply imitating theirs.

If this sounds like you, that's okay! It's not a bad thing; it means that you are a very ambitious person who wants more for yourself. As my mother says, *you must open all the doors of opportunity. You never know until you try.* The point I'm making is that in a world where everything is at our fingertips, it can be easy to forget our morals and values. You may redirect just to get lost again. Again, there is nothing wrong or bad with this, but getting to know your values is the best way to avoid getting lost on the journey we call life.

This is an excellent start to getting to know your values. If freedom, travel, and working remotely is what you want, that's great! Now you know that you can base your decisions on having a life and job with flexibility. You can pick a job or start a business that you can take with you, aligning with your morals and values.

Look, I am all for trying out new things to find your purpose, but the main issue in these stories is that people look at what others have, like the idea of the outcome, and don't enjoy the process or listen to what they truly want to do or like. People often seek the next best thing, *searching for their own purpose inside someone else's story*, without considering the process and only focusing on the outcome. However, the magic is in the process.

I've been a big fan of Gary Vee since I was a young teen; he always says, *"Enjoy the process."*

If you enjoy the process, you are winning in life; many people only think about the end result. Let me just add that if you are waiting for an end result:

1. *You are literally wishing time away and time = to life.*
2. *You will never achieve long-term happiness.*
3. *Life will drain the living soul out of you until you are an empty shell.*

Once you have reached that 'end goal', I can promise you that you will want something more. That's just how we humans work. It's like me saying, "I want to write a book," but every time I go to write, I can't stand it, or I'm not enjoying it, so… what's the point? This was me in my last business. I loved speaking with people, but carrying out treatments, booking appointments, and ordering stock was HELL! It's important to know what you're getting yourself into and whether what you are doing truly aligns with your values.

For many years, I faked loving the process. All the books I read said the same thing: love the process. So, instead of tuning in to my intuition and listening, even though it was screaming at me in many ways, I chose to ignore it and fake it and guess what…. It didn't work. While I am also a big fan of 'fake it till you make it, this is how I gained the confidence and guts to do the things I do and have done, but you can't fake purpose or fulfilment. These come from somewhere more magical than thought; they come through feeling!

Here are a few questions you can journal on:

1. If money didn't matter, what would I do?
2. Do you know your core values? If not, what are they?
3. Do you listen to your intuition? If not, what is your intuition, your higher self, trying to tell you?

Now, what happens when we go against our values, lie to ourselves, and ignore what our intuition says? We create resistance within us; everything becomes a chore, unenjoyable. It feels like life is stealing our souls day by day; many people will blame life or the people around them. That's okay. I did the same for years, and it wasn't until I took full responsibility that I figured out my values.

I now know what makes me happy and what choices I should make to serve my higher good! You don't need to be self-employed to do this. If you've done this exercise and your job doesn't align with your core values, my advice is not to pull yourself out of a stable income to soul search. What I'm saying is to start to become aware of what is in your life that no longer serves you, then make small steps to achieve your desired outcome. If this is a real struggle for you, hiring a life coach or a mentor may help you. You deserve to be fulfilled, and you deserve to live the life you truly want, but you will never get there until you work out your core values.

'Searching for their own purpose inside someone else's story.'

ANCESTRAL TRAUMA

'Healing from ancestral trauma is not just a personal journey, it's a generational one.'

From emotional behaviours to thought patterns and even beliefs around money, so much of what we carry has been passed down through generations. My ancestors lived in poverty; they struggled, worked endlessly, and received very little in return. They were looked down on by those in higher classes and made to feel small and unworthy.

When my nan was growing up in the 1930s, life was so different from today, from war, scarcity of food and space, and no support for those with nothing. The stress they endured didn't just vanish; it left a mark, one that's still felt today.

Ancestral trauma is real, and for a long time, I didn't even realise how much it was holding me back. But it is possible to see these patterns and break them. By healing ourselves now, we also heal the generations after us, creating a ripple of freedom and strength. This isn't just about our growth. It's about transforming the legacy we pass on.

Ancestral trauma is the pain passed down through generations because we are all made of energy and emit a frequency. When a family emits anger, unhappiness, suppressed emotions, etc., children can feel this and sometimes grow up still having the capacity to feel this (these people are often empaths), as you already know.

Families from different generations will pass down their negative, low, and suppressive energy to their children. On top of that, we have all been conditioned, so behaviours that are exposed to children will eventually be unconsciously copied. Ancestral trauma will continue to be passed down until you acknowledge it and change it.

My spiritual teacher Jane said, "The year 2024 is the stronger year, energy-wise". There is quite literally a shift in energy, which means people are becoming aware of their past traumas, conditioning and the, let's say, 'fakeness' that we live in. We have become so disconnected from the earth and nature. I hope this chapter helps you.

'Breaking the cycle of inherited pain is the key to finding peace in a modern world filled with noise.'

The future of our planet and future generations lies in the hands of us and the generation ahead; when we heal our trauma, we heal all future generations.

We now understand that we've all been conditioned in some way; if our parents or even their parents carried unresolved trauma, that energy is passed down to us. If we don't heal our trauma or the trauma that's been handed down, we'll inevitably pass it along.

The reason so many of us feel lost, broken, depressed, angry, and sad is because of our ancestors' trauma, maybe because they were beaten up as children, survivors of wars, or poor to the point they couldn't eat. They have *unconsciously* passed their pain onto us because they never looked deep into their minds and 'fixed' all the 'broken' pieces. It's now up to us to pick the pieces up and heal.

I spoke to my 94-year-old nan the other month while we looked through old pictures; she told me how she lived. She had nine sisters and brothers, and her dad was run over and killed when she was little; her mum had to move out of their home as she could no longer afford it and ended up moving into a two-bed house. All the sisters slept in one bedroom in one bed, and the boys slept in the scullery on the floor with bed sheets made from old rags.

I then remember my mum telling me what her childhood looked like. They had bricks for hot water bottles and metal rods they would stick in the fire to curl their hair, and they only had hand-me-down clothes. I remember my mum telling me that when she was younger, she would go to work with my nan at an all-boys boarding school, where she was a matron (a second mum to all the boys). My nan always told her that the people she served were rich and had more authority than them; they were to be looked up to as she felt they looked down on her. Don't get me wrong, my mum was happy as a child, but hearing this made me think deeply about my childhood. I started to realise where our deep-rooted money problems came from.

After my nan finished explaining her childhood, I asked about her mum's childhood; she, too, had many children and was extremely poor. I asked my nan if she thought that our long chain of poverty was because of the teachings our ancestors passed down to us. She stared blankly, as it was obvious no one had asked her that question. She agreed, and at that moment, I knew I had to break the chain of all ancestral trauma.

I started to realise that the cycle of financial struggles wasn't just about money. It was about the deep-rooted beliefs and behaviours passed down through generations.

My mum's experiences shaped how she viewed the world, and my nan's experiences shaped hers. This is why I still, to this day, have money blocks that I'm working on knocking down. But then I began to wonder: what else had been passed down? Not just in terms of money but in how we show up emotionally and mentally in our lives.

Screaming at kids, showing anger, or constantly complaining about life - what is that doing to a child? Not only does it traumatise them, but it also plants the seeds of those same behaviours for future generations unless someone chooses to break that pattern. You see, the chain isn't just about poverty; it's about the emotional responses we inherit, the mindset, and the way we interact with the world.

When we moan about life instead of showing gratitude, what's that teaching our kids? It's teaching them to focus on what's missing instead of appreciating what they have. And that cycle? It repeats itself unless we decide to step up and break it.

My dad would always say to us as kids, "I was beaten up, not brought up". It gave me such a different perspective on how grateful I was for my life. Don't get me wrong, my childhood was not all happy, but I couldn't be more grateful that I was not physically abused simply for being alive. My dad learnt that behaviour was no way to bring up a child; he understood that that chain couldn't be passed down. I could finally start to understand my dad's strict and unhinged behaviour due to his upbringing, and now only is it my and my brother's choice to flip the switch and break the antenatal trauma that we faced as children.

There are some aspects of our modern day that are causing more harm than good, and it would be best if we started to become aware of them now. Yes, we are physically safer than we were a hundred years ago. Our lives are much easier than ever before: we have running water, hot water, and electricity, but there is an epidemic happening that is not keeping our future generations mentally safe.

Humans have existed for around 300,000 years, and the internet has existed for over 40 years to date. Even though my family has a long history of poverty, their childhoods were spent being children and playing outside. Why are more children and young adults sadder than ever? Social media and screen time…

In the last 40 or more years, the internet has brainwashed and enslaved billions of people. Enslaved people to stay indoors and watch a screen. People are so blind to this because it has now become their comfort. Even though I was still brought up around the internet and social media, I think I was one of the last generations not to be glued to their phones or compare myself to 'influencers' and people with massive amounts of cosmetics and filters.

Children should not be stuck to a screen; it not only steals their childhood, but studies prove that it dumbs down their minds. They're calling it 'digital dementia,' but

it's not actually a condition. It's just what they're calling it because too much screen time can lead to memory issues, trouble focusing, and other dementia-like symptoms. It doesn't mean you're getting dementia, but it does show how excessive tech use can affect your brain. I'm not here to judge or put down anyone's parenting, but becoming aware of this is very important; as I said, the internet has only been a short amount of time compared to how long humans have been here, and the damage it has already done to many is sad.
We do not belong inside. Plants, trees, and air all have healing properties; they can and will heal us from many physical and mental illnesses.

In my town, crime has increased by over 30%. I'm not saying there's one cause, but it's hard to ignore how things like violent video games and certain trends in rap and 'trap' music could be influencing behaviour.

When I was in school, the boys would get into fights, but it was nothing like what's happening now. Kids from my old school are now carrying knives, and even 12-year-olds are walking around with weapons. This wasn't the case when I was at school around 10 years ago. It makes you wonder, what changed?

I'm not sure if many people know this, but public schools were created to produce employees who were not creative.

Kids go to school from 5 years old, sometimes younger. They are told what to wear in the UK at least, what to think and what not to think, what is 'wrong' or 'right', taught most things that don't matter, and made to sit in a classroom all day with only 30 minutes to an hour outside.

They are told what subjects to learn and, even worse, are graded and put into categories of intelligence. Is it just me who sees this as unnatural, unhealthy and damaging for the next generation that will then have an impact on the world we live in? The school system was created to produce mass employees, not create free entrepreneurs.

If you are interested in learning more about this, I recommend the book *Weapons of Mass Instruction* by John Taylor Gatto.

Like others, I had never fit in a classroom setting. I was 'different' and proud to be. Ask any of my teachers. I did not want to be told what to wear, what to think, and how to act, so you know what… I didn't. Did I get in trouble? Hell, yeah! But I knew deep down I was being true to my authentic self. Many of my 'issues' in school mainly

reflected my home life. My point is I was told that I was too dumb, too stupid, too naughty. I was told I was a failure because the school system didn't fit me. These places tell children that if they do not fit in the box laid out, they will amount to nothing…
Well, I am proof that that is a big fat lie!

I am dyslexic, yet I still managed to go to university and set up three separate businesses before 25. I then found enlightenment and woke up to the modern world. I am now a writer and life coach, and I am inspired to help millions of people around the world. Just because I didn't fit in their system, it in no way meant that I was designed for failure; if anything, I believe my life and life lessons have enabled me to help others.

In my opinion, kids are meant to be learning outside about nature and plants, not tied up to a desk; no wonder so many kids suffer from ADHD. They are not living the way humans were born to. This is entirely my perspective, and I hope it helps you see that our job in this world is to allow children to be children and not slaves to society and screens, as children are the future.

To date, I have no children, only fur babies, and there was a time I told myself I would never have kids because of our world. Then someone told me, "People like you are meant to have kids, as they are the future of our world."

I'm not naturally maternal toward children, only animals; we have this saying in our house, "Have cats, not kids!" but I feel like she had a point.

If I ever had children, I'd have 'hybrid' children. Aware of the modern world but exposed to the natural world. I personally would do anything to homeschool my child and make sure they are living, not existing. To teach them about gratitude, meditation, mind, body and spirit, how to grow food, treat animals, and have true empathy.

You can break the chain of past generations' beliefs, traumas, and thought processes. The first step is admitting that you do not know everything and investing time in your personal development. It quite literally starts with us.

'It only takes one person's words to move the perspectives of many.'

HEALING FROM THE PAST

'Our past does not define you. It prepares you.'

Once I started to forgive myself, my family, my thoughts, my conditioning and my beliefs, that's when true healing began. Deep down, I was still that hurt little child who needed to feel heard, comforted and loved. And then it hit me: the only person who could give me that love at the level I truly needed was me.

So, I began letting go of the pain, the stories and everything else I'd been holding onto that no longer served me. I released what weighed me down; from that moment, the healing started and hasn't stopped since. It's an ongoing journey, but I'm finally giving myself what I've always needed, which changes everything.

Healing from life's pain isn't just messy. It's uncomfortable, raw, and often downright painful. Life isn't easy, and it's not supposed to be. People and animals we love will pass on, relationships can end, and we might face broken bones, illness, or even emotional and physical wounds.

But here's the thing: healing doesn't mean erasing the pain. It's about learning to carry it differently, to grow through it, and to let it shape you without letting it define you.

Life is full of pain and suffering; you will be knocked down time and time again, but there is no time or energy to waste moaning about who knocked you down and why. You get back up time and time again because that's how we not only create success for ourselves but become stronger and more resilient.

Sure, moping around and feeling sorry for yourself might feel good in the moment; we've all been there. But let's be real: is it actually helping in the long run? Is it moving you closer to the life you want or the person you want to become? Probably not.

Feel the emotions and process them, but don't unpack and live there. You're capable of so much more than staying stuck.

And as Patrick Ness, an American-British author, says something a little similar to this:

'It's not about how you feel; it's about how you pick yourself back up.'

Healing begins when you realise that inside you is the child version of yourself, still craving love, understanding, and care not just from others but from yourself, too. Take the time to nurture, support, and hold yourself because when life throws challenges your way (and we all know it will), you need to be strong enough to handle them on your own terms.

Just because you have healed from one thing doesn't mean your journey is over. The healing journey is infinite; we are always learning, growing, and going through life-changing events, but what I see a lot of people do is hold on to their pain and past stress. Like I said in previous chapters, holding onto stories from the past steals your life and happiness, especially when you identify yourself as your story.

When I was younger, my parents were constantly at each other's throats; the tension grew so intense that, eventually, the police got involved. I lived close to my school, and let's just say my home life wasn't a secret; it was known by pretty much everyone. Even though I never played the victim, after my house was raided and the whole event spread on social media, that became my story. I wasn't old enough to even understand what healing meant back then.

Unconsciously, I let that event define me, and because I identified so strongly with it, I resisted healing. To me, healing felt like I would have to let go of the story that had shaped me for so long. It felt like it would erase a part of me, like tearing away the identity I had unknowingly attached to that pain.

This might be what's happening in your life, too. At one point, I even forgot a lot of my past. Was it PTSD? Fear? I believe I started forgetting because, on a deep level, I wasn't ready to heal. Healing meant detaching from that story, from the identity I had unknowingly attached to it.

'Turning my pain into my identity.'

'If I'd known that this beautiful, caring soul was buried behind all that trauma, I would have faced it a hell of a lot sooner.'

I had this light within me, but it was hidden behind walls I didn't even realise were there. That was my journey. I may not understand why everything happens for a reason, but it just does. It's not our job to know or understand why. Our job is to do the best with what we have been given.

I no longer look back at what happened to my family as a pointless, painful experience. Even though it was painful then, the awakening of the results and skills that came after are priceless. And I will forever be grateful for the pain and the healing that came later in its own time. Don't put pressure on yourself; you may not be ready, or you may be pushing yourself instead of allowing it to flow.

Things happen to us, or how I like to say 'for us' empowering, disempowering, negative, and positive; this is something I wish my 13-year-old self could hear.

Every event is here to teach us something, and it's up to you whether you hear and understand the lessons or ignore and blame the world, your teacher, parents, partner, and or the universe.

Learn from everything!!

When Peach, my kitten, got killed, life itself felt over, worthless, useless, and for months, I was racking my brain: why, why, why? I couldn't understand why this had happened and for what sick reason, but the truth is we learnt so much from Peaches. For some reason, we gave her so much love, more love than our other Maine Coons. For the one year and three months she was here with us, the attention was on her. We loved her unconditionally, as if we were going to lose her.

The thing is, we had to heal from that, especially what I felt the days following. My point is that we learned from this.

Love like there is no tomorrow because there might not be. Even the most beautiful things don't last; become aware and listen to your senses and feelings.

Healing from the past means accepting what has happened, turning the pain into power and accepting that you cannot change it. What you do from now and the decisions you make will create your future. It's about understanding that you have a choice. A choice to let go, heal and move on. This does not mean to forget; it just means to let go of the emotional hold it has over you.

Like I said before, your pain could be your greatest power if you make the choice for it to be. What you have gone through and your experiences may help another; your healing WILL become infectious. And if I had known that this beautiful human was behind the trauma, I would have healed a hell of a lot sooner.

THE TRUE AWAKENING

'A true awakening begins when we realise that the power to change our lives lies within our own minds and hearts.'

Well, we're nearly at the end of our journey together, and by now, you've learned a lot about self-development, mindset, and the journey that's brought me here. People often ask me, "When did you wake up?" or "When did you have your spiritual awakening?"

There are two answers. One was the day after my Auntie Netty passed away. That moment hit me hard. But it wasn't just that one moment; it was every lesson, every experience, every tool and insight that built up to that wake-up call, spiritually, physically, and mentally. Every ounce of pain, every story, and every setback contributed to my awakening. And, honestly, I'm grateful for it all.

Even though some memories still bring me great pain, without my pain, you wouldn't be holding this book right now.

So, when did I wake up? The truth is, I've been waking up since the day I was born. And so have you. It's just a matter of the perspective you choose to see it from. We're all on this ongoing journey of awakening, one moment at a time.

The conscious brain is responsible for awareness and perception. It processes information from the environment and the unconscious mind, influencing decision-making and rational thinking.

I used to think I was 'woke' because I meditated, wore cool Buddhist-printed clothes, and collected crystals from a young age. It has nothing to do with any of those things because they are all (other than meditation) external. I would moan, argue, get angry, and become irritated daily. Waking up means coming out of your world and seeing the world as a whole, a collective. When I am happy, the world is happy because we are all connected through the frequency we emit. When I spread happiness and joy, that is infectious; the same goes when I am down and depressed.

Feel these statements:
- Every day is a blessing.
- Every moment is beautiful.
- Everything that happens to you is teaching you something.
- People are temporary.
- Things are temporary.
- Life is temporary.

When you start embodying these statements, remember them and live by them. Life begins because you understand that we have such a limited time here, and there is no time to waste your energy on moaning, being negative, angry, or sad. Of course, feel your feelings, but let go of them before they consume you.

For all we know, we have one life, f*ck the past, heal and move on; allow the energy to flow and don't allow the past to hold you back or weigh you down. For the time we have left on earth, make choices that not only align with you and your true purpose but also bring you joy. Take on whatever resonates with you in this book and many others you read. It's okay if you don't know what your purpose is; usually, our purpose is the thing that makes us happier and fulfilled.

Learn these statements, embody them and feel them
- Love, like there is no tomorrow.
- See everything like there is no tomorrow.
- Travel if that's what you want.
- Spend time with family and friends.
- Spend time alone, being with yourself.

Simply do, like you could be gone tomorrow. I know it is a scary thought for most, but being scared of the fact that tomorrow isn't a promise does not make it any less true; it will only hinder your time here.

Life throws us sh*t, people we love die, tragic stuff happens, and hard times come out of nowhere. But if you let that stuff define who you are, it takes over. When you let your past stories become your identity, you're setting yourself up for a life that's miserable, unfulfilled, and lacking gratitude.

When you start to see the bigger picture in life, notice and embody the patterns that you're seeing. You can then start to manipulate the world and shape it into what you want. This is because we only see what is happening in the outer world through what is happening within us.

When we change the inner, the outer will start to change, too; the thing is, nothing is really changing. The world is still the exact same place; the only difference is your perspective, making the outer world look so different.

Happiness, freedom, and money are all out there; instead of searching for it in the world, start to *FEEL* it within you. Only then will you begin to see the opportunities.

Every morning, you wake up, and you see that you have a choice. The ball is always in your court; you choose how you react to situations. I used to live in a mindset of blame. Everything that was happening was happening *to* me, but now I understand that everything is happening *for* me, every struggle, hurdle and challenge. Yes, it may be hard and painful, but my perspective is now, 'this is happening for me' to teach me, to make me stronger.

Tony Robbins made a good point in one of his talks: the world has always had these problems: war, violence, and financial inflation. The only reason it affects us more now than ever is because we see it all day through our phones. Going back fifty or more years, all these things were still happening, but they just weren't shoved in our faces all day via social media, so they didn't have the power to affect people and their perception of the world.

That's exactly why I don't let it mess with my energy. The truth is, whether I feel sad about it or not, it doesn't change a thing; it's still happening. But letting it take over my emotions and my day? That's on me. To live as the best version of yourself, you've got to tune out the constant stream of negativity, focus on what lights you up, and spread good energy wherever you can. Stay focused, keep your vibe high, and put your energy into building the life you want, not reacting to the chaos around you.

Stay focused, stay in your lane, and put your energy into building the life you want, not reacting to the chaos around you. Because here's the thing: when you realise that true happiness comes from within and not from anything external, life stops feeling like survival. It starts feeling like living.

I truly hope this book has helped you and will continue to create a mindset that makes you feel freer, happier, and more at peace with whatever life throws your way.

The Final Chapter:

MIRACLES ARE HAPPENING

'A miracle is simply a shift in perception when you choose to see the beauty in what's already here.'

Whatever you choose to believe will become your reality. *We as humans are all floating on this massive rock called Earth while other floating rocks surround it... in a world full of unexplained mystery, make a choice to believe in miracles!*

I will start with an actual study before I jump into my miracle story.

The study took place in 2011, and it's called 'The Rice Experiment - How Your Words Create Reality'
The short and simple version of this study is that Dr. Masaru Emoto got two bowls of boiled rice, both from the same packet and both boiled at the same time.
He spoke negatively every day to one bowl of rice, and to the other, he spoke positively. The bowl of rice that was being spoken to negatively went mouldy quicker, whereas the other bowl that was being spoken to positively didn't; anyone can try this experiment at home. All you need is two bowls of rice and some patience. This literally proves the power of positive words and MIRACLES!

I heard about this study when one of my cats, Baloo, got sick. Hold your hats, ladies and gents; it's about to get really sad, but luckily with a happy ending. This story is truly one of my biggest miracle stories, and it still makes me feel so powerful and magical when I think about it.

Around a year after Peaches passed away, Peaches's dad, Baloo, got sick out of nowhere. Little did we know how bad it would get. One day, he came into my room after an evening of being a typical Maine Coon, when I noticed he had lost his voice. During this time, I had tonsillitis, and I thought that I had given it to him (it's okay to laugh all you want; the vet certainly did!)

We took him to the vet the next day when we noticed his nose was bone dry and he couldn't eat. His nose got to the point where it got so dry it turned into a scab and fell off. The vet told us it was probably some cat flu, gave us some meds and said it should go within the next week.

As the week went on, Baloo's condition got dangerously worse; in the space of nearly four weeks, he had gone from a very healthy, happy Maine Coon, weighing around 6kg, to skin and bone. He lost over half of his weight; he couldn't eat, drink, or open his eyes. Despite going back to the vet and having follow-up blood tests, everything was coming back to normal.

Baloo was finally referred to a specialist cat clinic called 'The Oxford Cat Clinic', with the best vets we could have asked for. After a lovely lady called Martha checked

Baloo, she was sure that he had an extremely rare disease called 'Dysautonomia'. In simple terms, his normal bodily functions had stopped working. Martha began to tell us that less than 20% of animals survive, and due to Baloo having pretty much all the symptoms, we should very much consider that Baloo wouldn't make it much longer. He was on death's door. I wish I were exaggerating. He was starving, literally starving. He wanted to eat so badly, but because his body not producing saliva and his body not being able to turn food into poo, not to mention he was unable to chew properly, you could feel and see his bones through his fur. His eyes lost the ability to dilate and create tears to keep his eyes moist.

This was indeed a hell-on-earth situation for us. After having Peaches taken away, the thought of Baloo going too was unbearable.

Everyone told us to put him down; the vet said most animals don't survive, and if they do, they are challenged with a lifetime of deadly side effects. Month two, and Baloo was not getting any better; he would cry all the time for love and would sit on us anytime we were home. During this time, I had an operation to have my tonsils removed. My surgery went wrong, and I ended up in the hospital for an extra week; I, too, couldn't eat or sleep and was drugged up on medication. The pain of being so hungry but unable to eat hit home; I started to realise a little bit of how Baloo was feeling. My partner and I had the conviction to put Baloo to sleep until... one of my clinets told me about the rice study.

This was the last thing to try; his meditation wasn't working, he still couldn't eat or drink, and his life was hanging on by a single thread.

Every day, every moment we had with him, we were constantly healing him. I would put my head on his head and say, "You're a healing boy, you're a strong boy, you're getting better each day." My partner made up a song he would sing to him every moment he could. When I tell you… He started eating, going outside, running, playing, and gaining weight.

From death's door to health, it was a f*cking miracle! We still 'can't' believe it; his recovery was proof, which happened just days after we started speaking positively to him.

Now Baloo is doing GREAT! Nine months later, we took him back to the specialist, and she was shocked at how well Baloo had bounced back, as she thought it was impossible.

Miracles happen, and the secret is the power of empowering energy and positive words.

Please use this story as pure motivation to achieve whatever you truly desire because even if you come from an extremely suppressed family, even if you have no one positive around you or even if you have been brought up in poverty, you can achieve anything you wish for if the language you use is empowering, positive and motivating. Only you can truly change what words you say internally and out loud. I have given you all the knowledge I currently have and have learnt along the way, but *YOU* must be the one to take *ACTION*!

We can experience phases of waiting: waiting for life to get exciting, waiting to heal, and waiting for life to start. But the longer we wait, the more time we waste staying in unsupportive, negative, and disempowering mindsets, and the more we waste our precious time here on earth.

Believing in yourself and having faith are all you really need. Don't limit yourself. You don't need to have perfect grades, a perfectly organised life, a picture-perfect family, fancy clothes, flawless hair, a bigger bum, or a smaller tummy to make it happen. If you've got faith in yourself, you can do whatever the hell you want.

You don't need anyone else's approval or faith in you, even though it's nice to have. As long as you believe in yourself and keep that faith, you'll always be winning.

Everything I've learned, the mindset shifts, the tools, the lessons that took me from rock bottom to the strong, mindful, and creative soul I am today, are now yours. As I continue to grow and discover more ways to live in alignment and thrive, you can bet I'll be sharing every bit of it with you.

So, until next time, my beautiful humans, keep living and loving with every ounce of your being.

Never forget...

'Tomorrow isn't promised.'

With love and gratitude,
Your Soul Sister, Pix

P.S

If this book has resonated with you and you feel ready to cultivate a powerful mindset and make real changes in your life, then you're already on the right path.

Join me on my social media platforms and check out Thrive Beyond Limits, my online coaching program.

I get it; I've been through it, too. And trust me, it's so much more beautiful on the other side. See you there!

Post your favourite page, quote or chapter onto social media and tag me, @pixiiwilliams and #youngdumbdepressedbook

Peaches

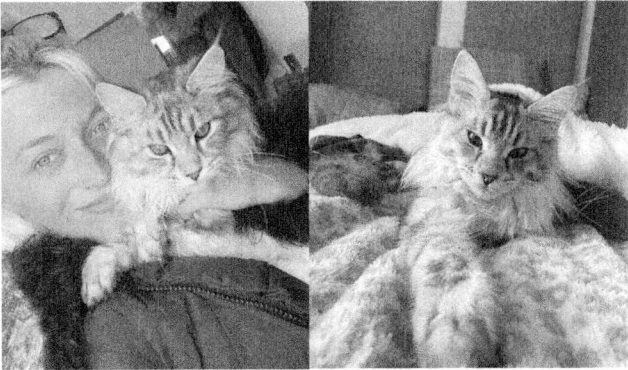

'Don't cry because it's over; smile because it happened.'

About the Author

Pixii Williams

is a mindset coach, writer, and entrepreneur with an unstoppable drive to break through blocks and create a life of true fulfilment.

Dedicated to helping others wake up and live more aligned, authentic lives, Pixii's journey of reconditioning her own mind to see life in a brighter, more empowering way has inspired countless people.

Through her coaching platform, Thrive Beyond Limits, and her growing social media community, Pixii is a beacon of light in the darkness, encouraging others to embrace their power and transform their lives.

We'd love to hear from you! Connect with Pixii on her social media platforms to share your journey and take the next step toward your best life.

f **○** **t** @pixiiwilliams

REFERENCES

Bessel van der Kolk. - The Body Keeps the

Darryl Anka Bashar. - Writer and Speaker

Gary Vee - Entrepreneur Speaker and Author

Tony Robbins - Author, Coach

Eleanor Roosevelt - Political Figure

Allan Watts - Writer, Speaker, Philosophical Entertainer

Dr. Masaru Emoto - The Rice Studie

"Cymatics: Chladni Plate - Sound, Vibration and Sand"

Patrick Ness - American British Author

John Taylor Gatto - Weapons of Mass Instruction, Autor, Educator

Printed in Dunstable, United Kingdom